funORIGAMI

8 Easy & Playful Projects
with 75 Sheets of Origami Paper
+ How-To Videos

DOVER PUBLICATIONS
Garden City, New York

This Dover edition, first published in 2026, is a new English translation of *Origami divertenti*, published by NuiNui, Switzerland, in 2021.

ISBN-13: 978-0-486-85563-9
ISBN-10: 0-486-85563-5

Printed in China
85563501 2025
www.doverpublications.com

Text and illustrations
Nick Robinson
Marc Kirschenbaum
Vanda Battaglia and Francesco Decio

Photographs
Dario Canova
Paolo Biano
Araldo De Luca

Translated from the Italian by Vali Tamm

When you see a QR code, use your smartphone or tablet to access a video tutorial. You can also access videos for each of the models by typing the URL below into your browser.

www.nuinui.ch/it/libro/strappa-e-piega-origami-divertenti/video

Table of Contents

Instructions

Selecting the paper

- Most origami models require square sheets of paper. Once you have used up the sheets provided with this book, you can purchase additional paper in craft stores or online.
- We recommend always starting out with a sheet of paper that is larger than required and then trimming it down into smaller squares. This is the most cost-effective approach.
- Origami paper is generally colored on one side and white on the other.
- To make the models in this book, we suggest using sheets of paper in a variety of colors and patterns. Select the ones you feel will be best suited to each of the models.
- We recommend that you test out each model using inexpensive paper before trying to execute the final product with higher quality paper.

Folding the paper

- Place your sheet of paper on a flat, solid, well-lit surface, such as a table, and make sure you have sufficient elbow room.
- Keep in mind that once a fold has been made in paper, it is almost impossible to remove the crease completely.
- Proceed with each fold very carefully. Don't rush through the instructions, and make sure to position your sheet of paper on your work surface in such a way that makes it easy to fold.
- When you are ready, take hold of the bottom edge of the sheet of paper with one hand and slowly bring it toward the top edge, using your other hand to hold the paper in place on the supporting surface.
- Once the two edges are perfectly aligned, start to flatten the paper by pressing down gently and sliding your finger in the direction of the intended fold with a light movement.
- Finally, to finish the fold and make sure it is clean and well-defined, go over the crease with a fingernail (usually the thumbnail).
- Many people prefer folding the sheet of paper in a direction away from themselves, rather than toward themselves, to avoid having their hands interfere with the folding.

Techniques

Name	*Symbol*	*Application*	*Result*
Valley fold		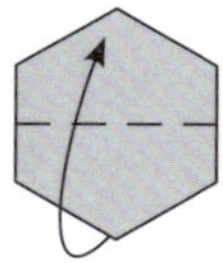	
Valley fold and unfold		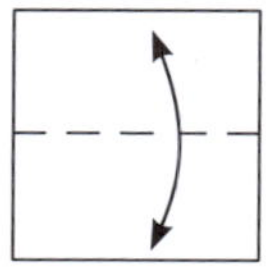	
Mountain fold		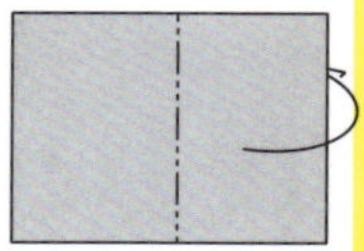	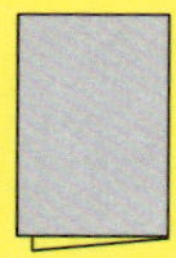
Mountain fold and unfold		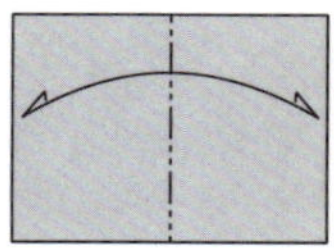	
Repeat the fold once, twice, three times, etc.	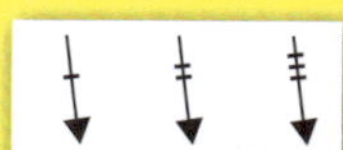	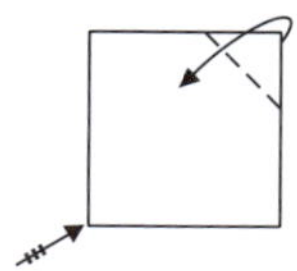	

Name	*Symbol* / *Application* / *Result*
Bring point to point	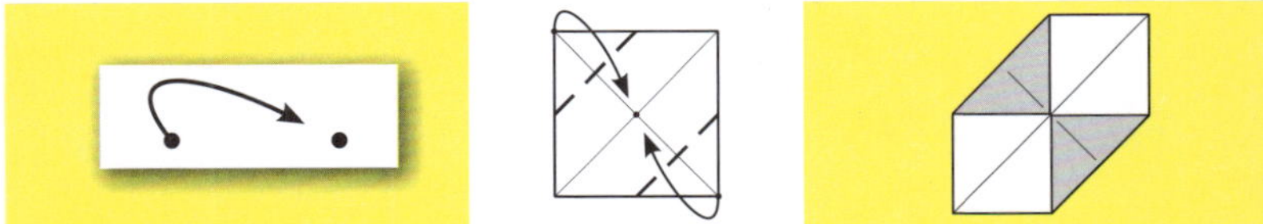
Fold behind or insert beneath a layer	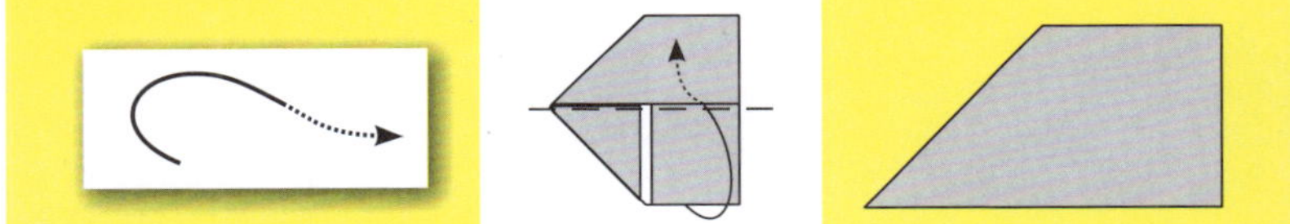
Hidden edges (X-ray view)	
Turn over	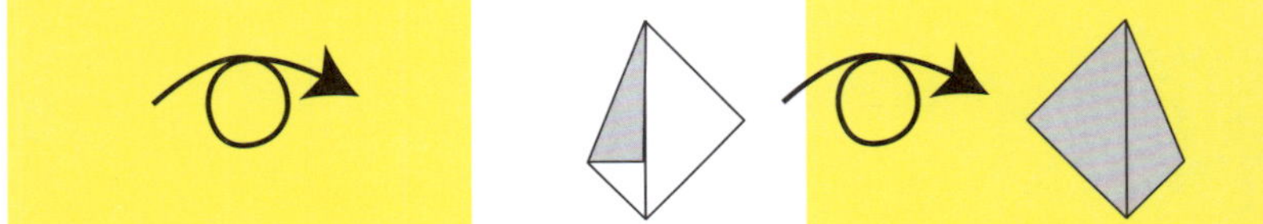
Push in, squash, sink a corner	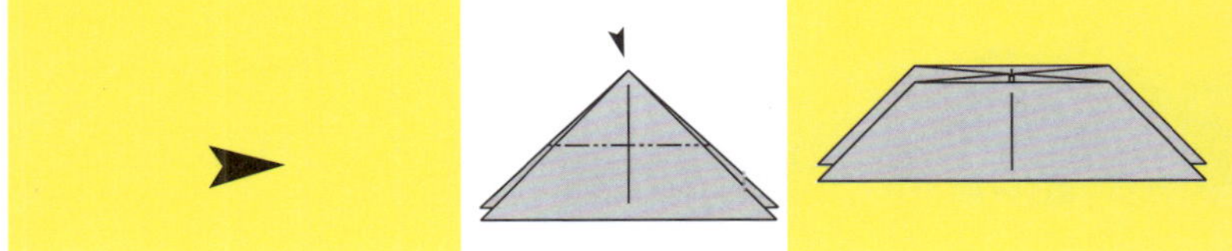

Name	*Symbol*	*Application*	*Result*
Rotate the model to change its orientation		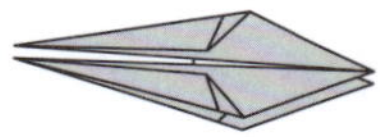	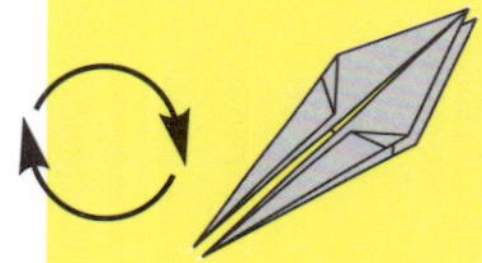
Fold the angle bisector		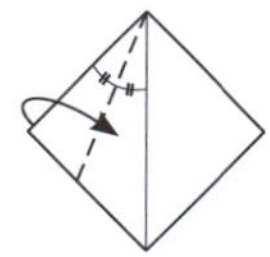	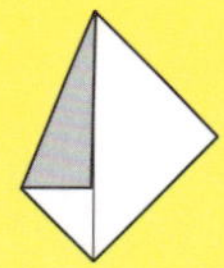
Pleat or accordion fold		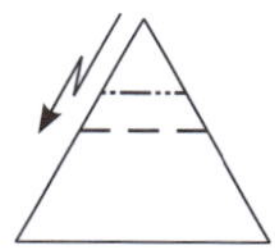	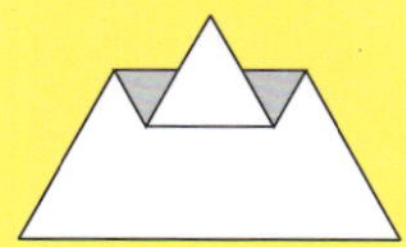
Inside crimp fold	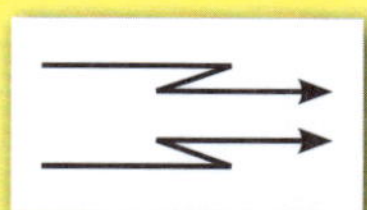	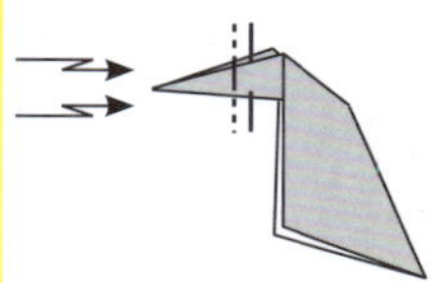	
Open out one or more creases or layers		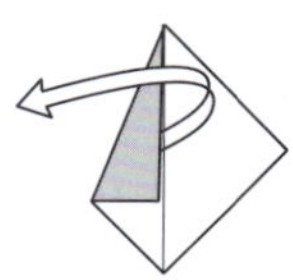	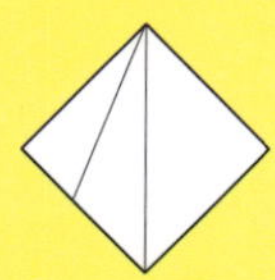

Name	*Symbol*	*Application*	*Result*
Zoom in		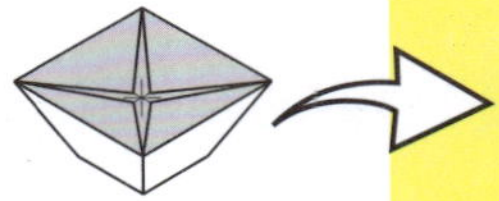	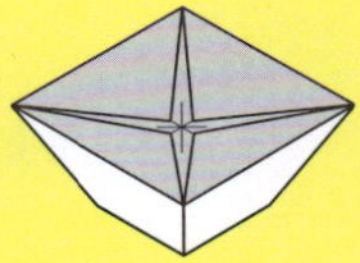
Zoom out		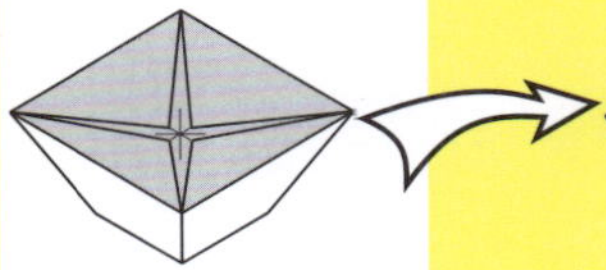	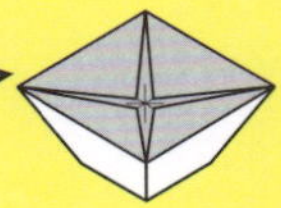
90° fold		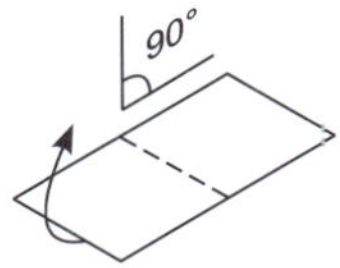	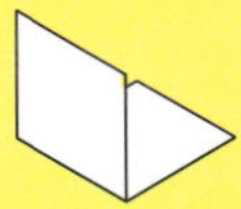
Inflate the model			
The model is three-dimensional	3D	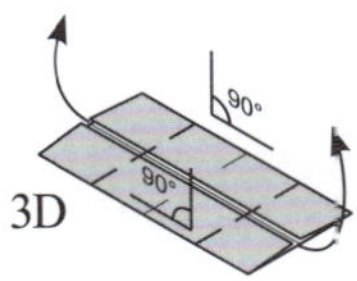	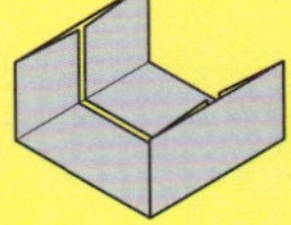

Scan for a video tutorial.

Sitting Cat: Rear View

Wayne Brown

Usually, origami models of cats present a front view. This model is unusual in that it shows the cat from a different perspective—one that is familiar to many of us!

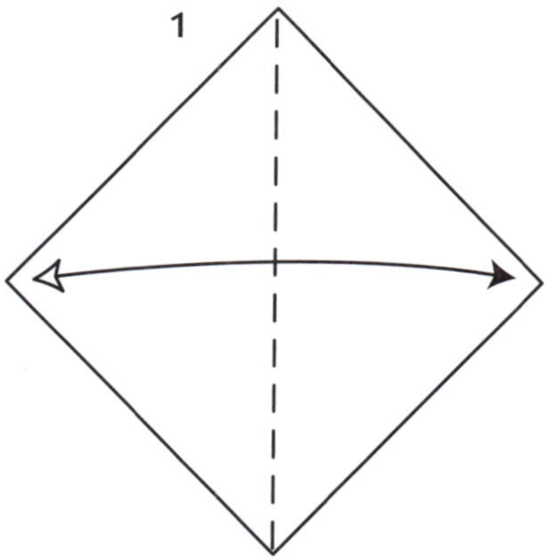

1. Fold and unfold the sheet of paper along a diagonal.

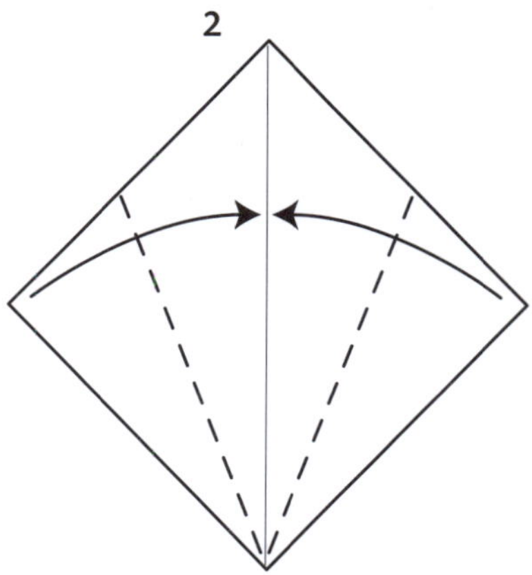

2. Fold each of the two lower edges inward, toward the center.

3

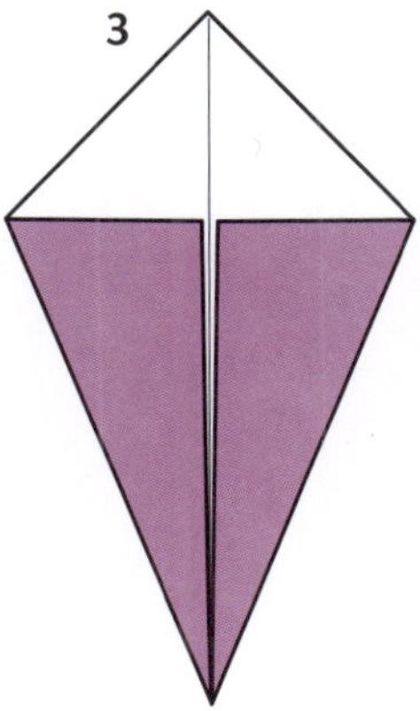

3. This is what the paper should look like. Turn it over.

4

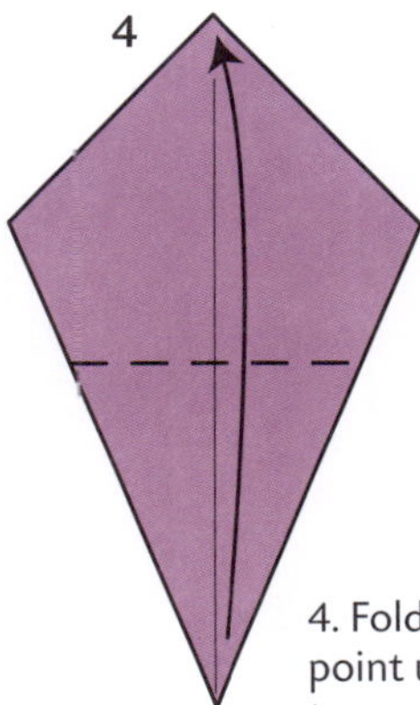

4. Fold the bottom point up onto the top point.

5

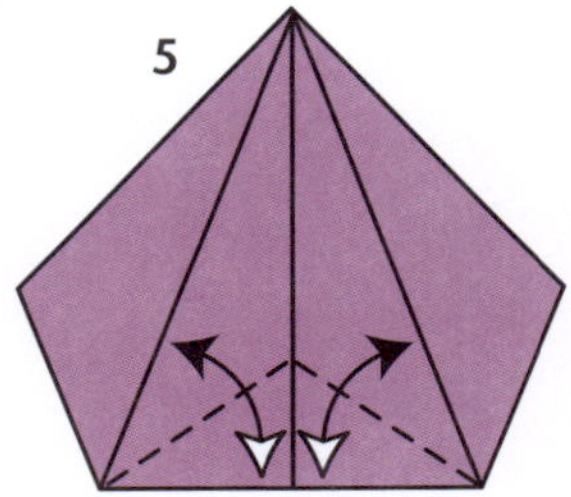

5. Fold the top left edge of the triangle on the left onto the base of the sheet of paper and then unfold the crease back to the original position. Repeat using the top right edge of the triangle on the right.

6

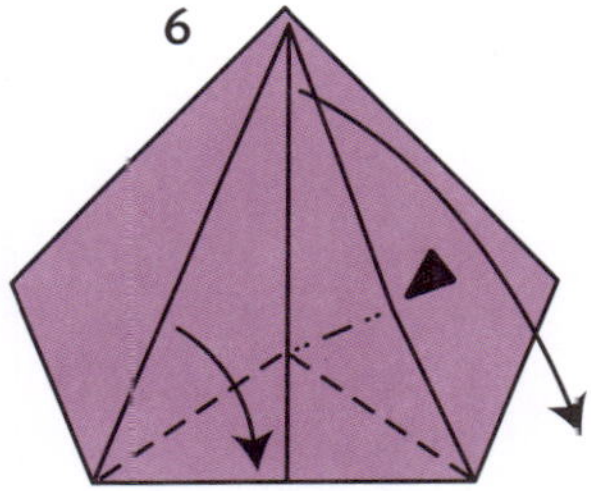

6. Pinch the two sides of the central triangle and collapse it to the right so its left edge lines up with the base of the sheet of paper, using creases as shown.

7

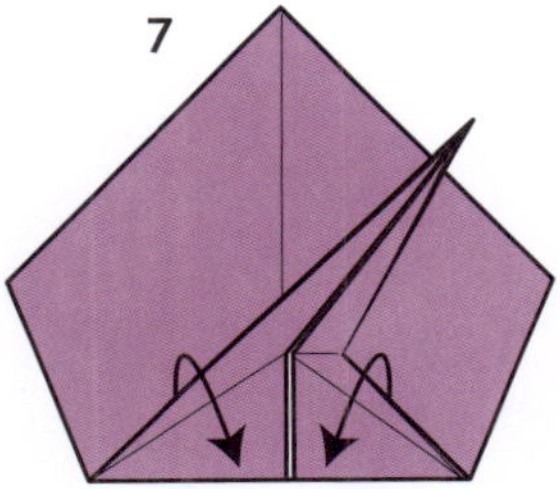

7. This is what the folding action should look like.

8

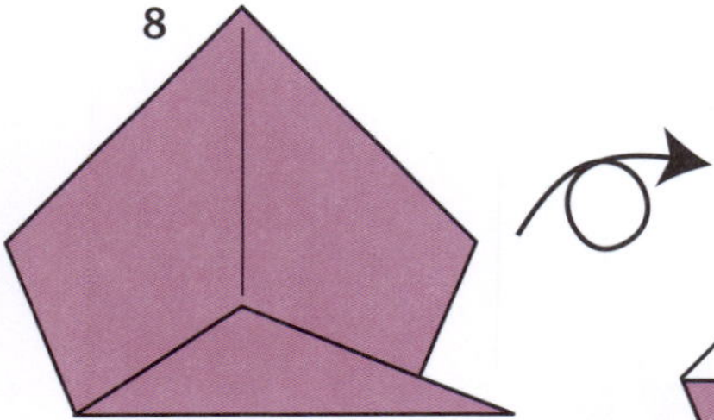

8. This is what the paper should look like. Turn the model over.

9

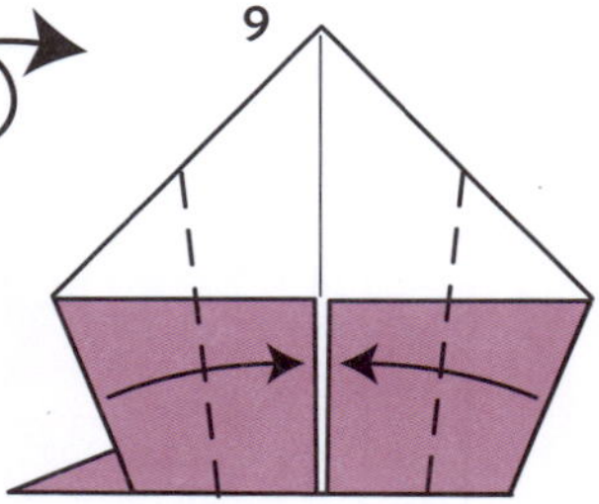

9. Fold the colored edges toward the center.

10

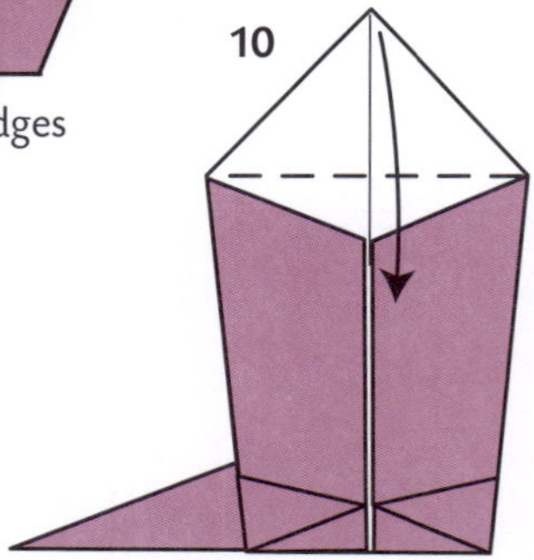

10. Fold down the top flap.

11

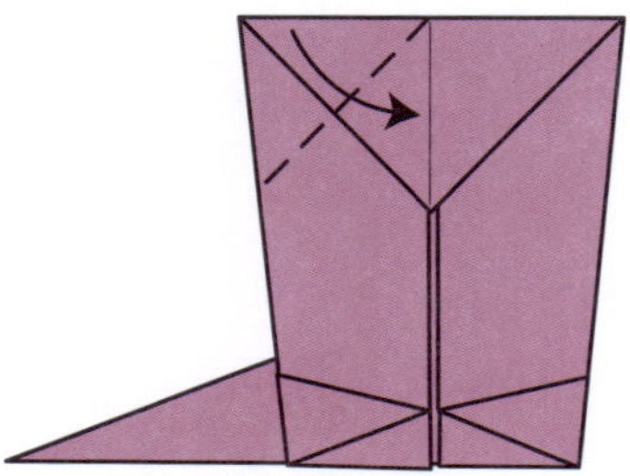

11. Fold the top left corner down toward the central axis.

15

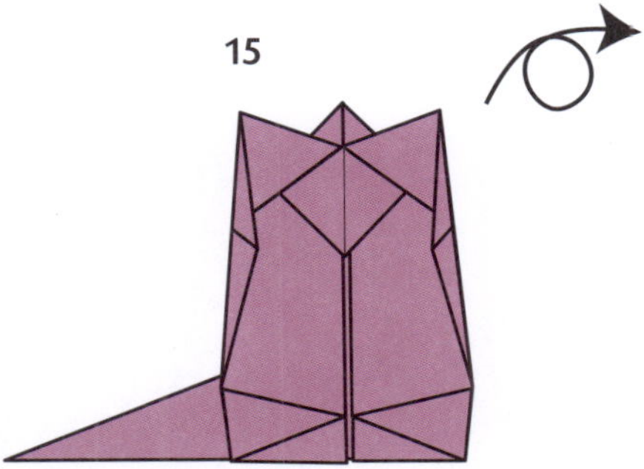

15. This is what it should look like. Turn the model over.

14

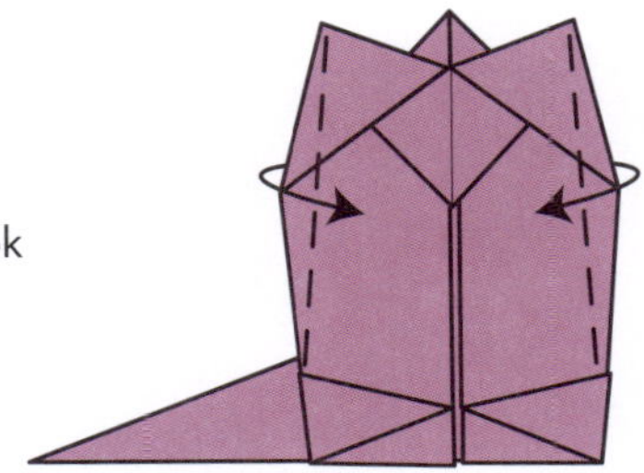

14. Starting with the top corners of the cat's ears, fold the left and right edges inward as shown.

12

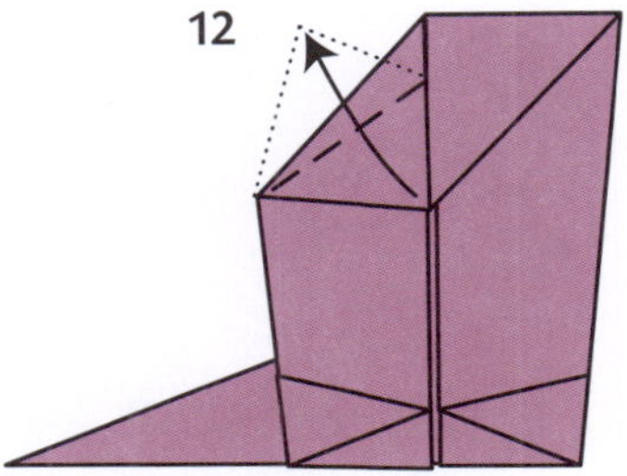

12. Now fold that same flap backward, as indicated by the dotted line.

13

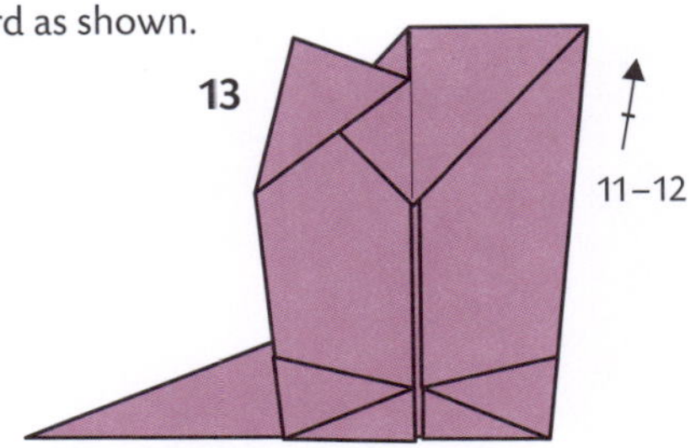

13. Repeat Steps 11 and 12 on the right side of the model. These are the cat's ears.

16

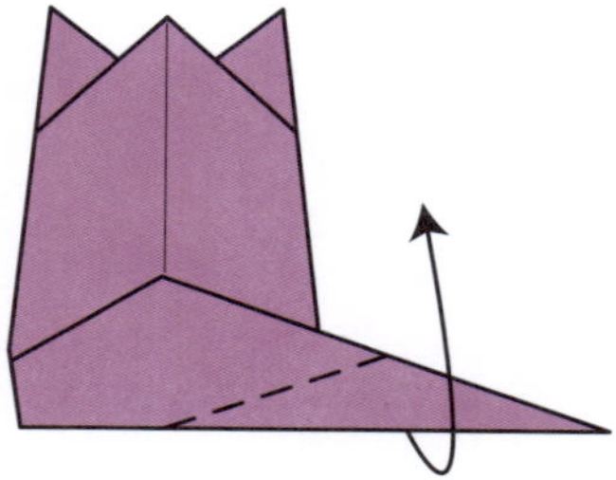

16. Fold up the tail.

17

17. Sharpen the tail by folding back a flap.

18

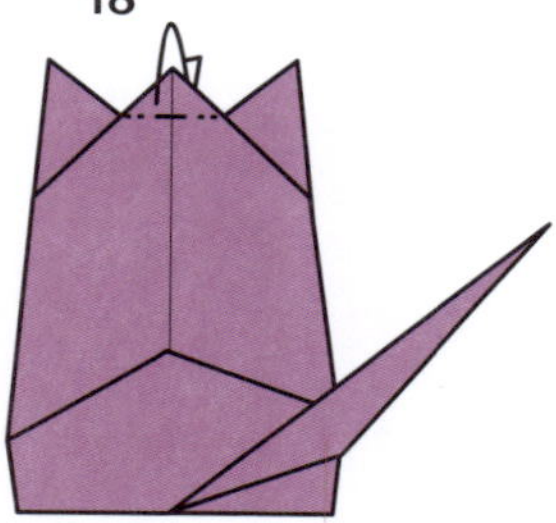

18. Fold down the flap that is between the ears.

19

19. The rearview model of the sitting cat is now complete.

Scan for a video tutorial.

Butterfly with Pinwheel Base

Traditional model

This model is created using a pinwheel (or windmill) base.

1

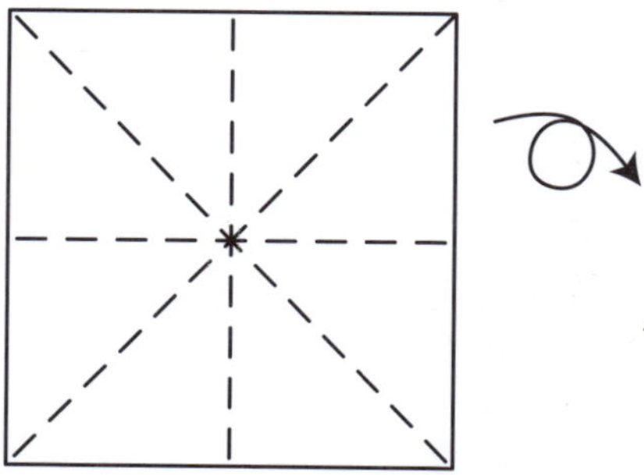

1. With the white side facing up, fold the sheet in half and then unfold it. Repeat three times, rotating the sheet at each turn to create creases as shown. Turn the paper over.

2

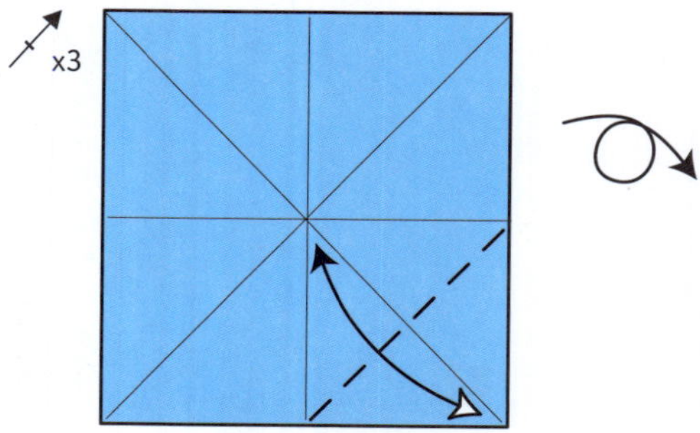

2. One at a time, fold the four corners in toward the center and turn the paper over.

6

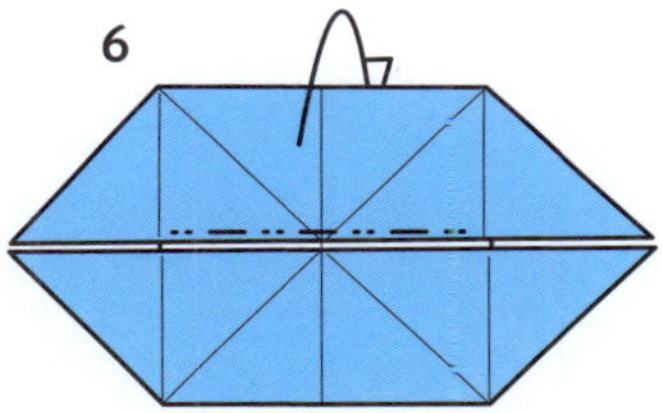

6. Fold back the top half.

5

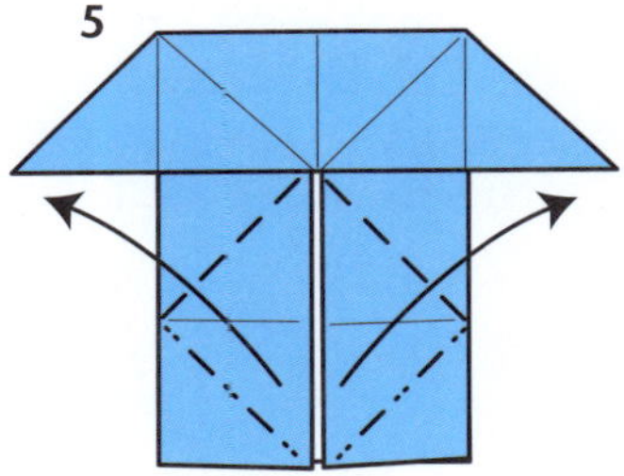

5. Repeat the last step on the bottom half of the model.

4

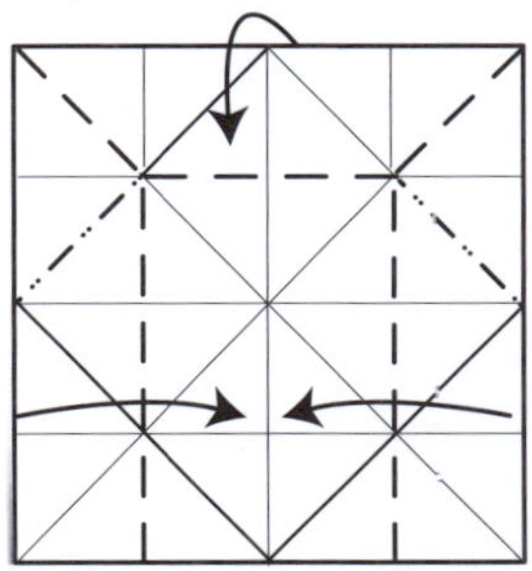

4. Fold the two side edges toward the center and the top edge down toward the center as shown.

3

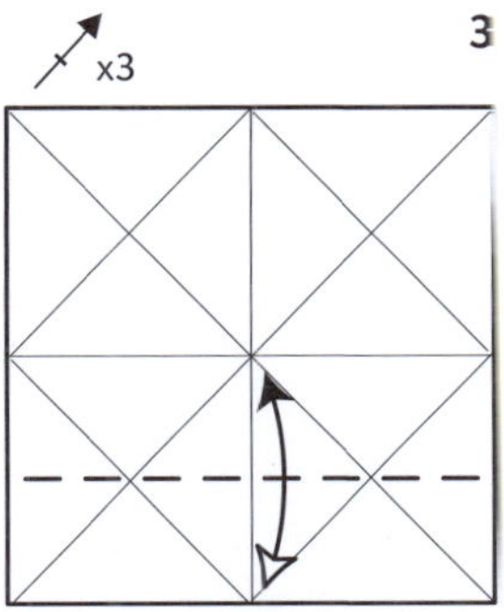

3. Fold the bottom edge up toward the center and then unfold. Rotate the sheet 90° and repeat the previous step. Repeat twice until the creases appear as shown.

7

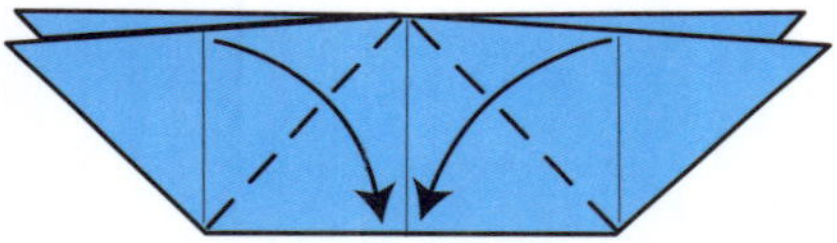

7. Fold the front two flaps forward, toward the base.

8

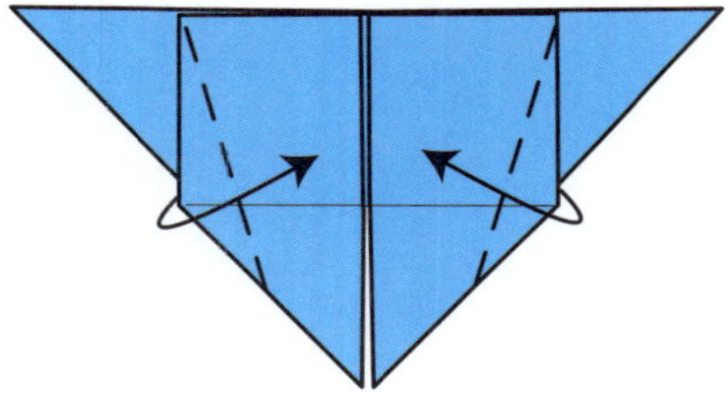

8. Fold part of the two outer edges of this new flap toward the center as shown.

9

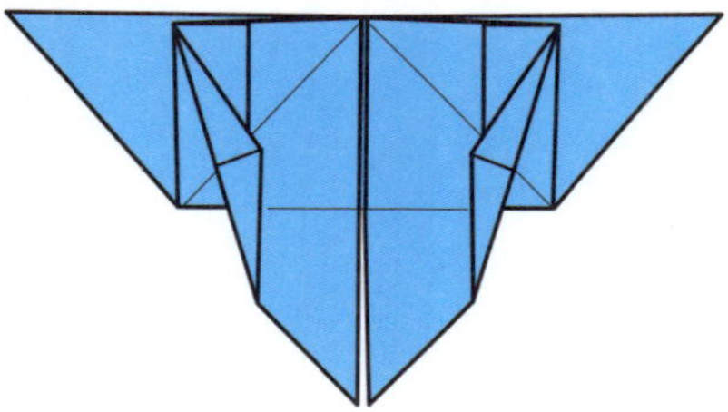

9. This is what it should look like. Turn the model over.

10

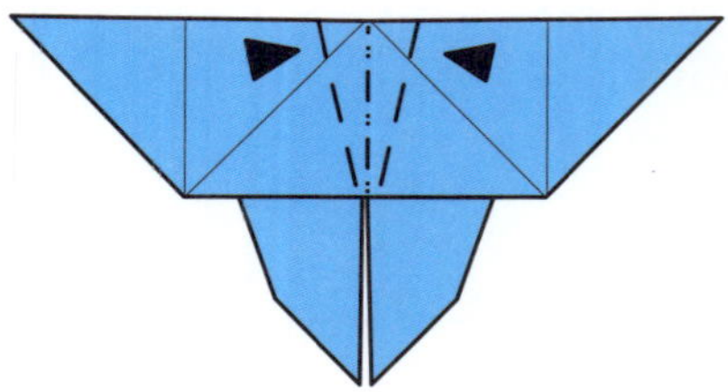

10. To turn this into a three-dimensional model, pinch the central axis as shown.

11

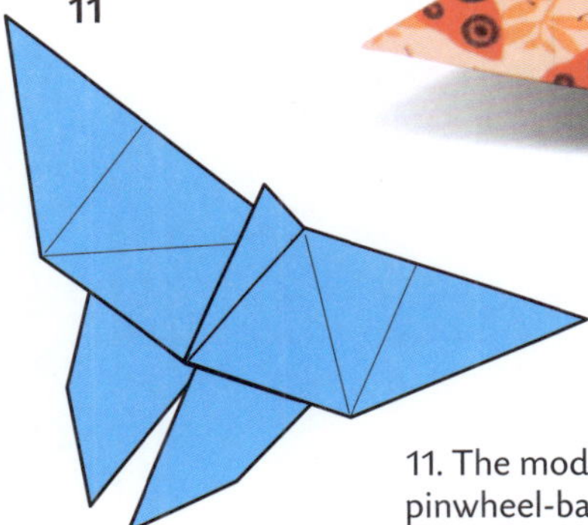

11. The model of the pinwheel-base butterfly is now complete.

Scan for a video tutorial.

Love Note

Nick Robinson

The perfect gift for the one you love.

1

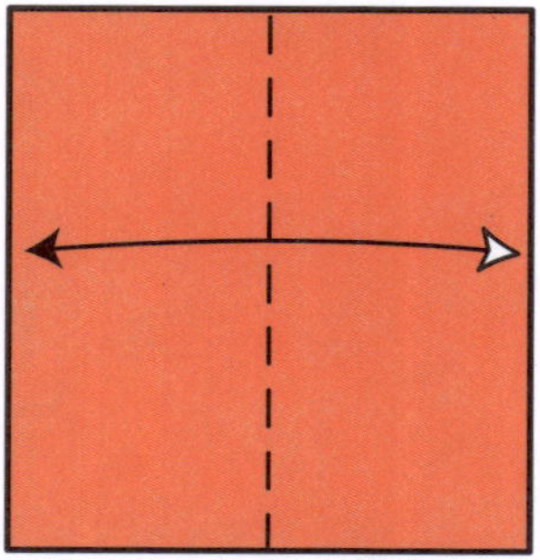

1. With the colored side of the paper facing up, fold the sheet in half, crease, and unfold.

2

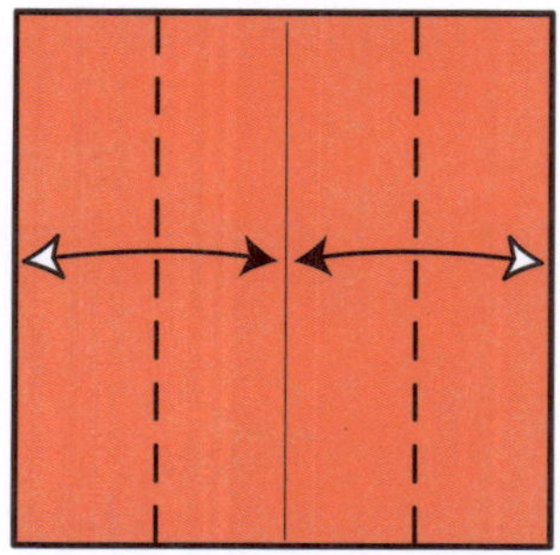

2. Fold each of the two sides in toward the central crease and then unfold.

6

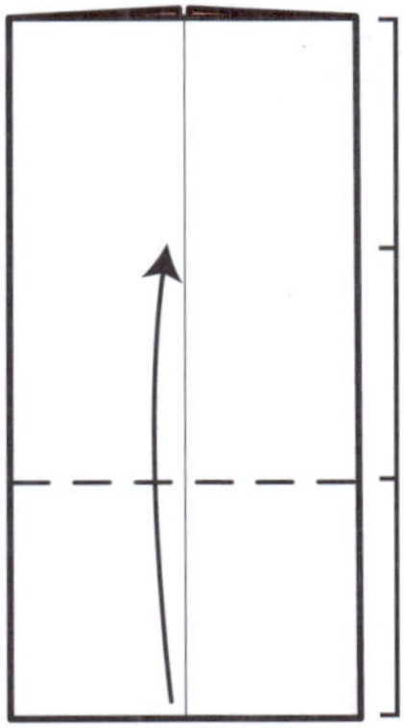

6. Fold the bottom edge upward, forming a crease about one-third of the way between the base and the top of the paper.

5

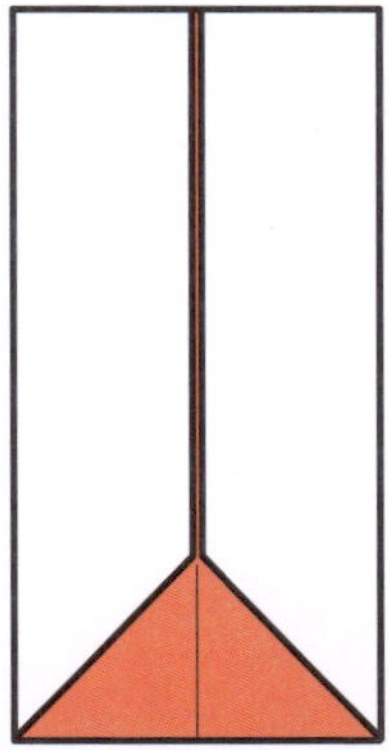

5. This is what it should look like. Turn the model over.

3

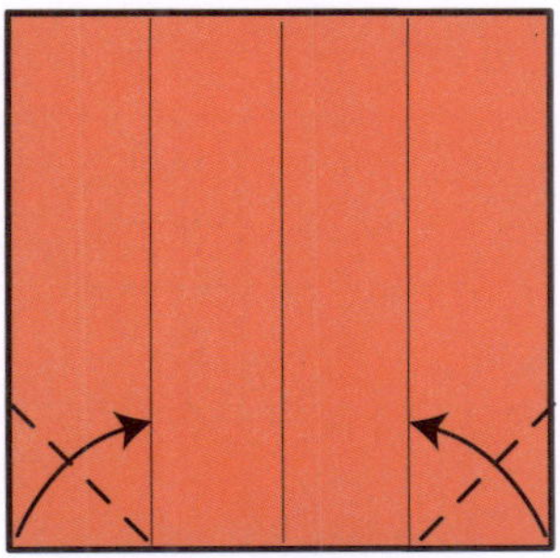

3. Fold the bottom two corners toward the two outer creases.

4

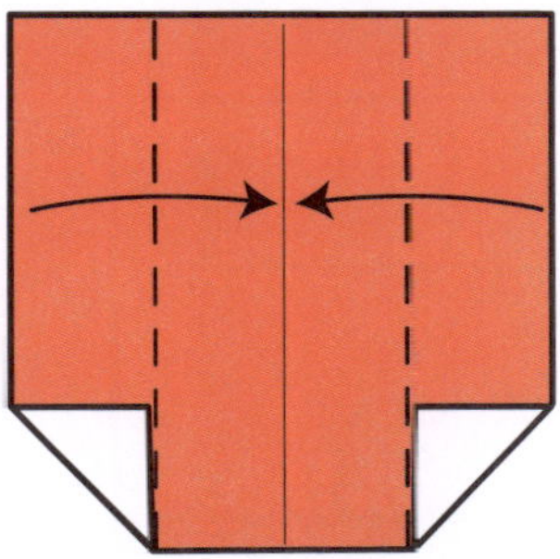

4. Refold the two sides toward the central crease.

7

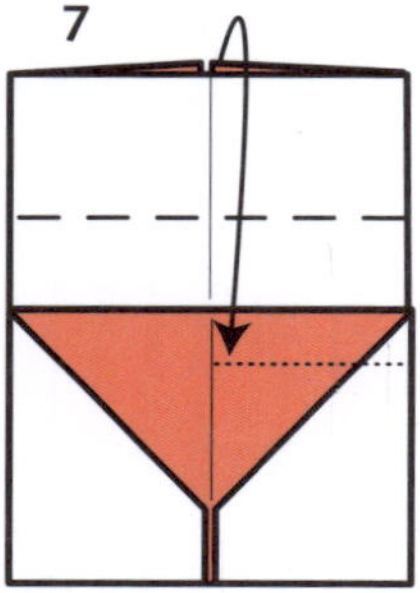

7. Fold the top edge down, using the dotted line in the illustration as a guide.

8

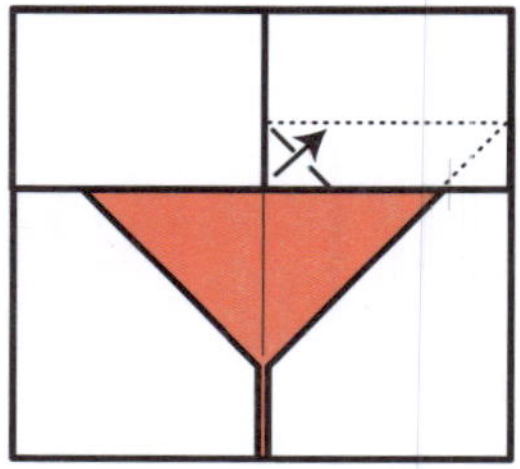

8. Starting with the right half, fold back the corner closest to the center line toward the dotted line.

9

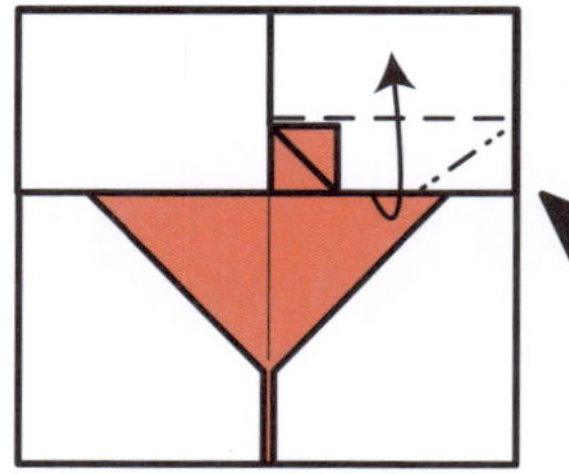

9. Using the top layer only, fold it back, toward the top, and flatten its rightmost corner along a diagonal (see the next step).

The slightly asymmetrical fold of Step 9 will create a flap long enough that it can be tucked beneath another layer to be secured. You can modify the shape of the heart with slight variations to Steps 3 and 8–9.

10

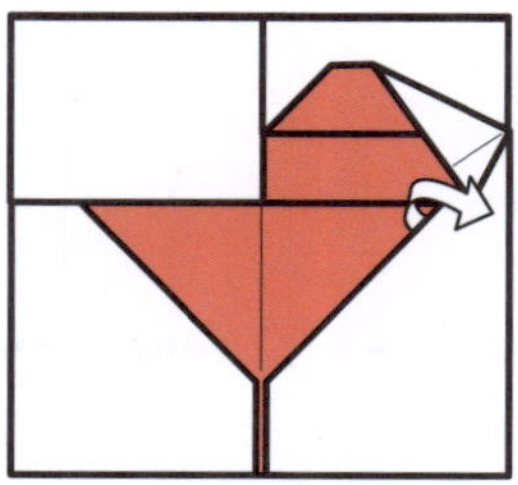

10. Using the tip of a finger, lift the top layer of the bottom right of the model and tuck the flap from the previous step into it.

8–10

11

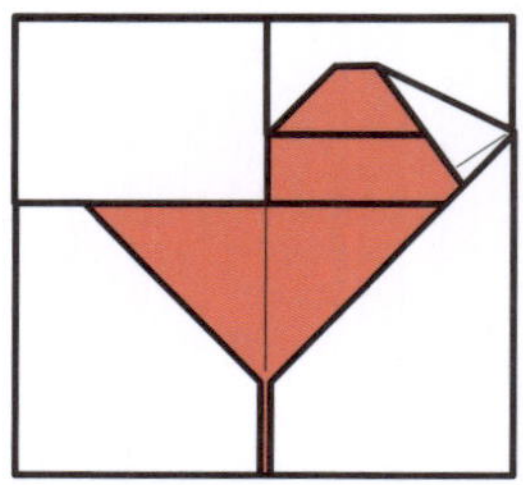

11. Repeat Steps 8–9 on the left half of the model.

12

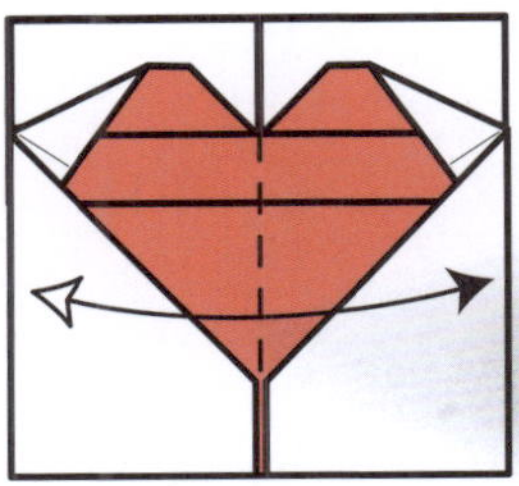

12. Reinforce the central fold. You can now close the note and present it to someone.

Scan for a video tutorial.

Cup

Traditional model

Through the techniques of origami, it is possible to reproduce any living creature in a folded paper form, as well as a vast array of common objects. The origami cup, for instance, is among the most popular because of its usefulness and simple design. It can be used to hold small objects and, if made using waterproof paper, can also hold liquids!

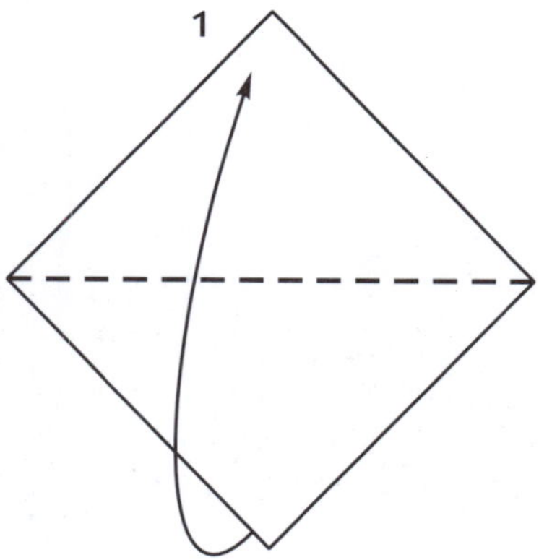

1. Fold the paper in half using a valley fold along the horizontal diagonal axis.

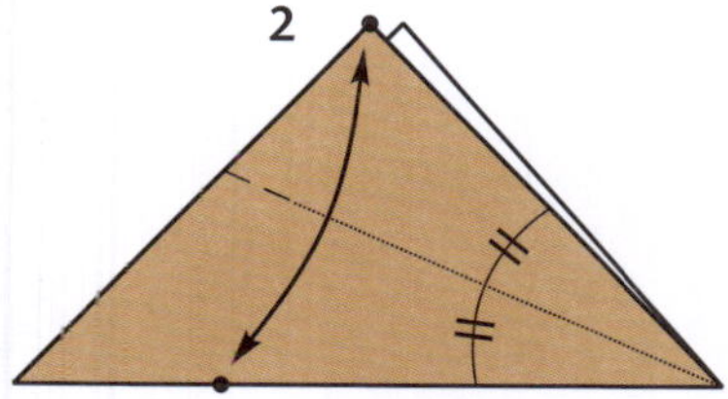

2. Fold the top layer back toward you, creating a valley fold. Unfold.

6

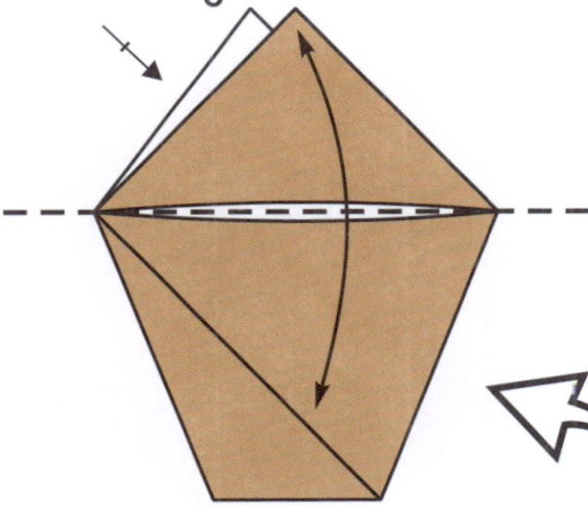

6. Fold and then unfold the top flap only. Repeat on the back side.

5

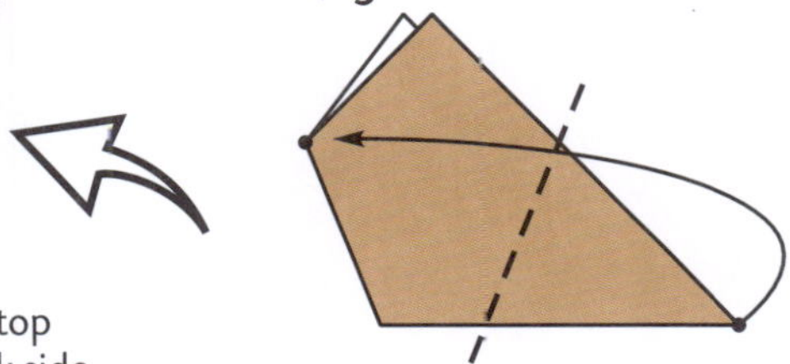

5. Flip the model over and fold the right corner onto the point indicated by the arrow.

4

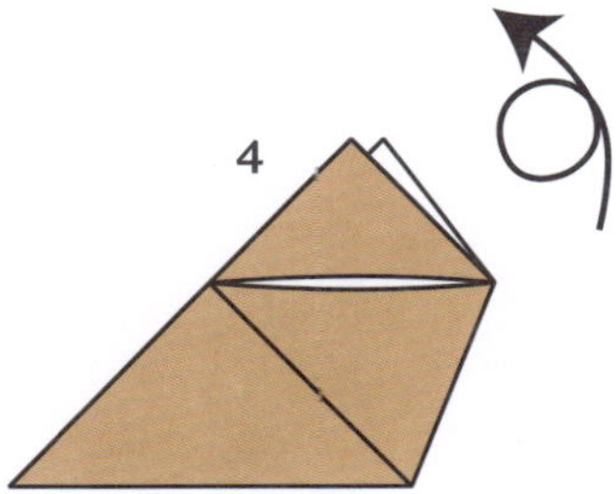

4. This is what the model should look like after Step 3.

3

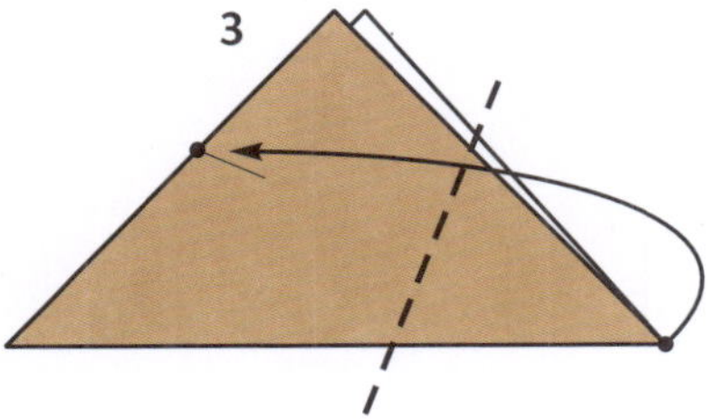

3. Fold the bottom right corner of the triangle leftward, so the corner meets the left edge of the crease made in Step 2.

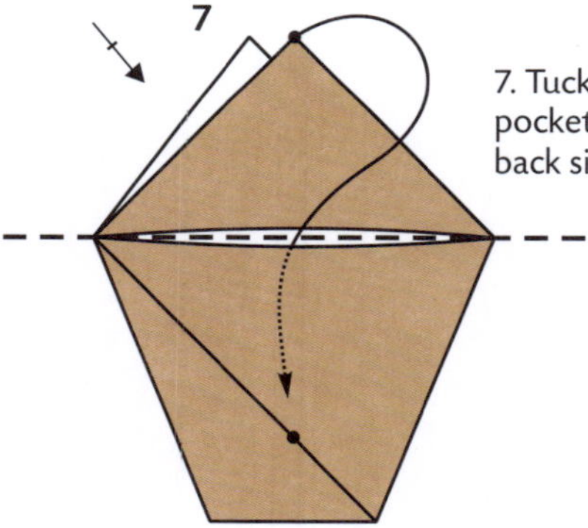

7. Tuck the top flap into the front pocket as indicated. Repeat on the back side.

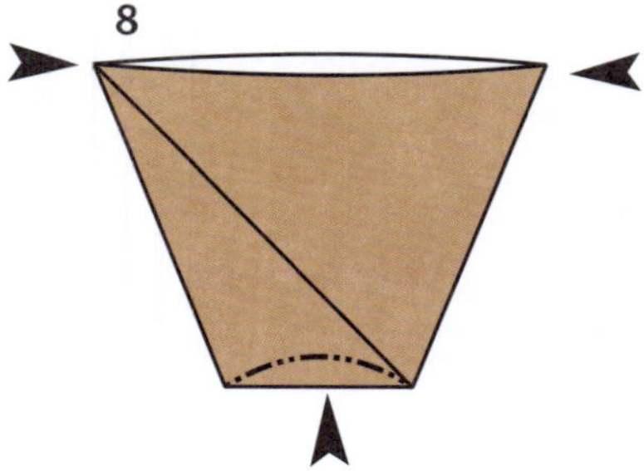

8. This is what the model should look like after Step 7. Adjust by widening the top part of the cup and gently pinching the lower part.

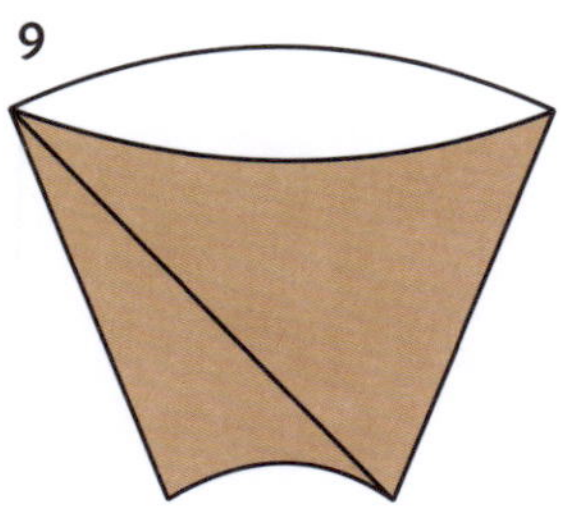

9. The model of the cup is now complete.

Scan for a video tutorial.

Simple Envelope

Traditional model

Just as a handwritten note can feel especially meaningful, so too does a handcrafted envelope become uniquely personal when it is made from a carefully chosen sheet of paper. By following these instructions, you will create an envelope that, while simple, will add an extra touch of originality to its contents.

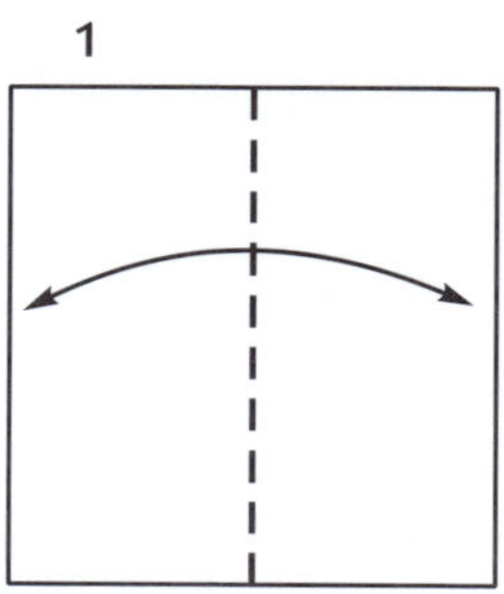

1. Fold the paper in half along the vertical median using a valley fold. Then unfold.

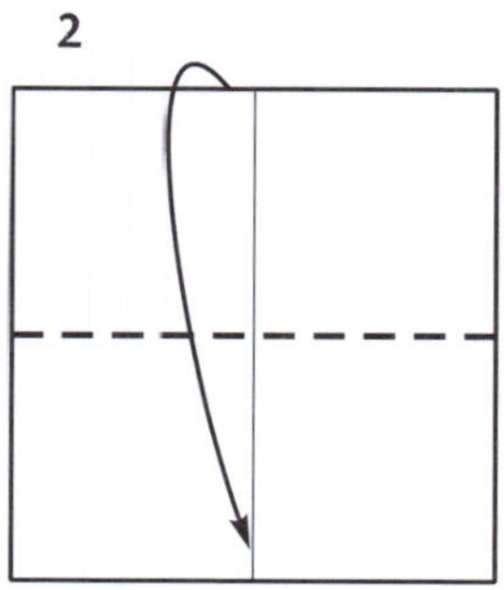

2. Now fold the paper in half using a valley fold along the horizontal median.

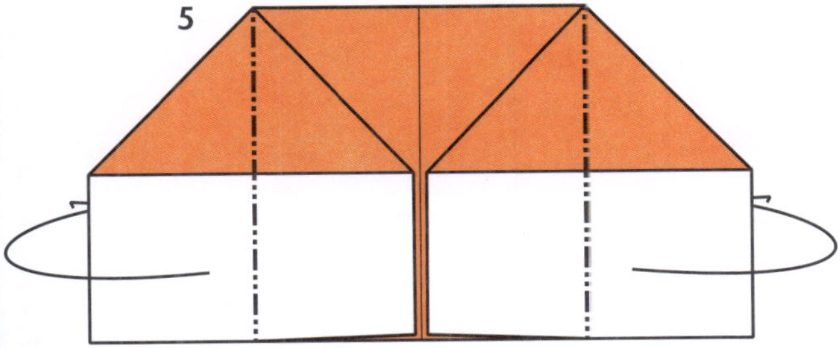

5. Make mountain folds on each side, as indicated, and fold the flaps to the back.

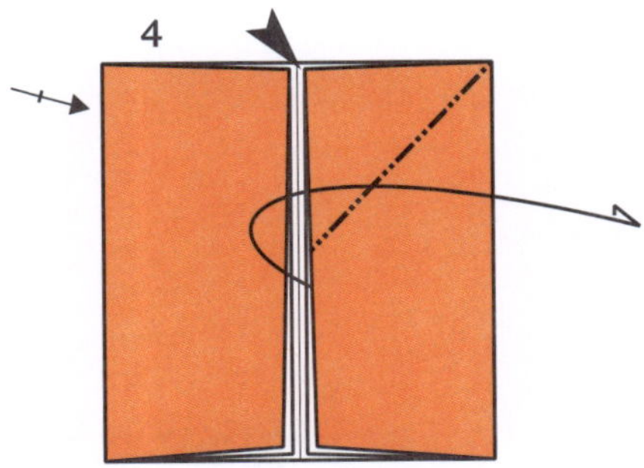

4. This image is enlarged for clarity. Fold back the top left corner of the right flap. Insert your finger through the bottom of the folded back layer, open it up along the mountain fold, and squash it flat as shown. Repeat on the left side of the model.

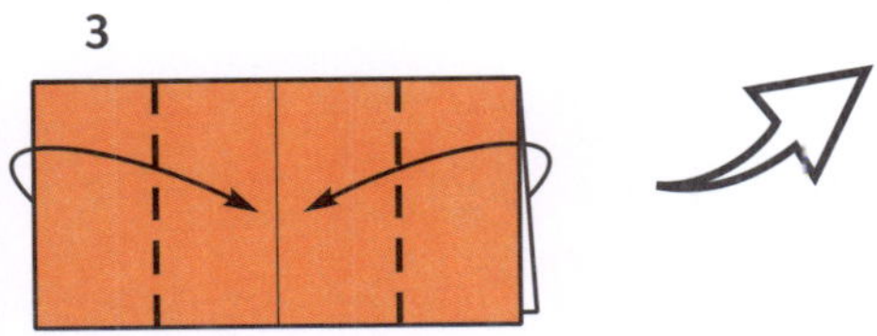

3. Fold the right and left edges inward, toward the center, using valley folds.

6

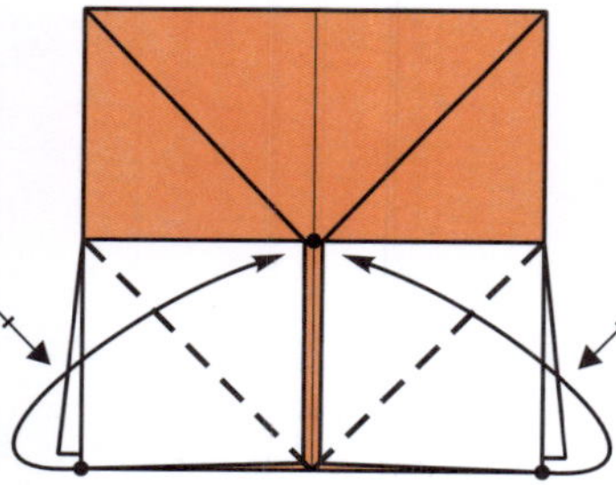

6. Using valley folds, bring the bottom right and bottom left corners up to the center of the model. Repeat on the back side.

7

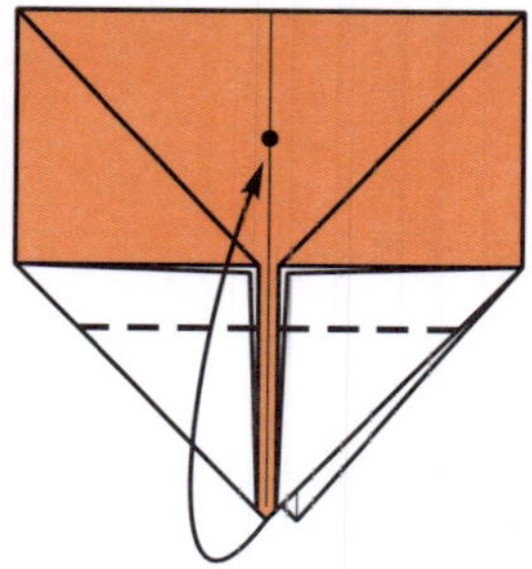

7. Using a valley fold, bring the apex of the top layer of the triangle up to the middle of the top part of the model. The fold does not have a precise reference point.

8

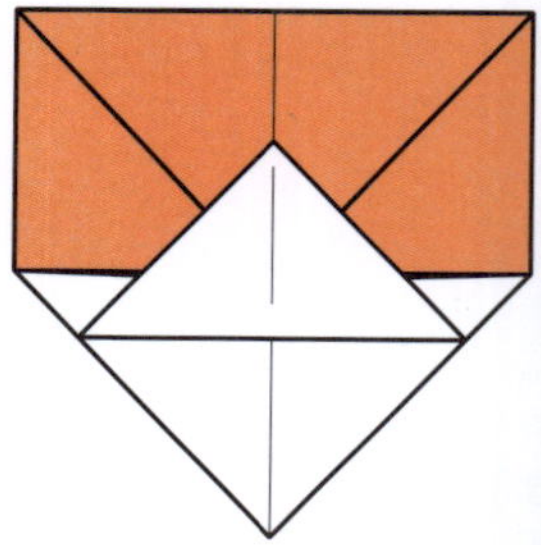

8. This is what the model should look like after Step 7.

9

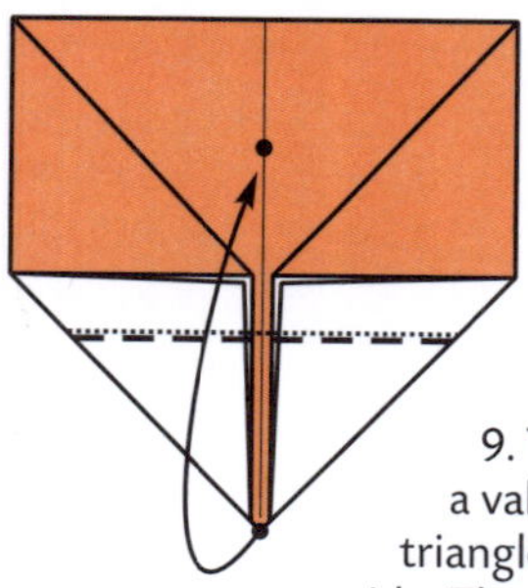

9. Turn the model over and, using a valley fold, fold the apex of the triangle as was done on the other side. The dashed line is a reference line indicating the fold line used in Step 8.

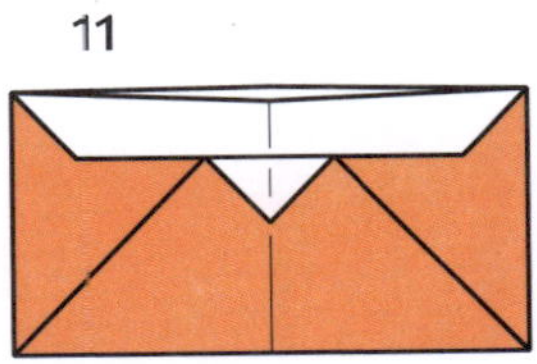

11. The simple envelope is now ready to use.

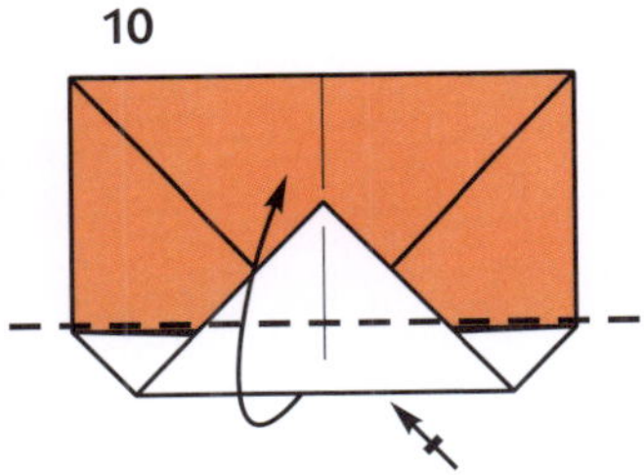

10. Use a valley fold to fold up the base of the model. Repeat on the back side.

Scan for a video tutorial.

Piano

Traditional model

Among the vast array of musical instruments, the piano stands out as one of the most fascinating, due in part to its ability to produce multiple notes simultaneously. In fact, some consider it to be the undisputed "king" of instruments. The origami version of the piano preserves the elegance that sets it apart, making it a truly unique and original model.

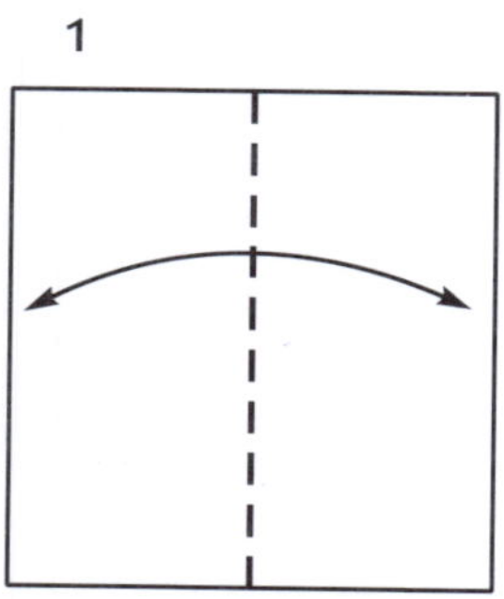

1. Fold the paper in half along the vertical median using a valley fold. Then unfold.

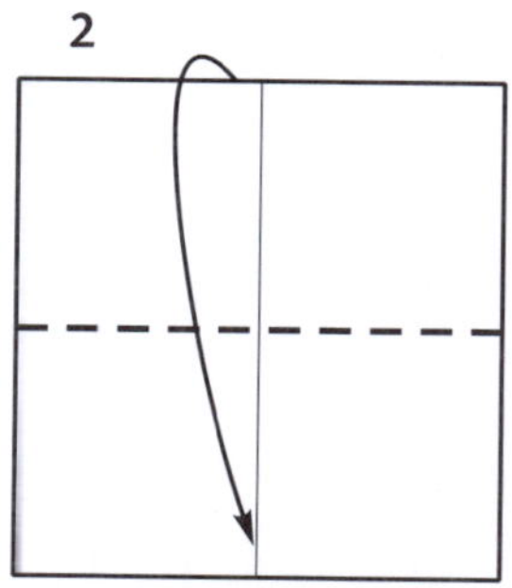

2. Now fold the paper in half using a valley fold along the horizontal median.

6

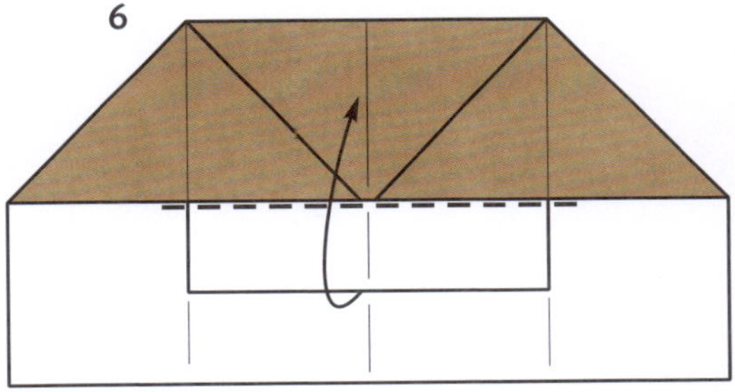

6. Use another valley fold to fold this flap upward again.

5

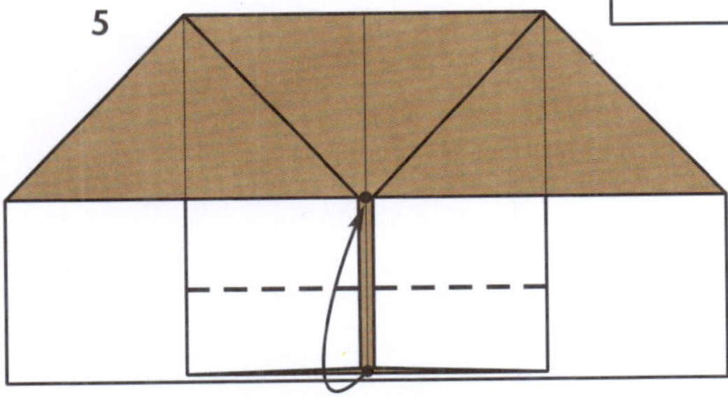

5. Using a valley fold, bring the bottom half of the top layer's flap up, coupling the two dots as shown.

3

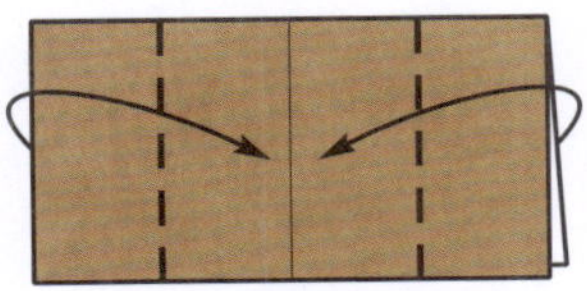

3. Fold the right and left edges inward, toward the center, using valley folds.

4

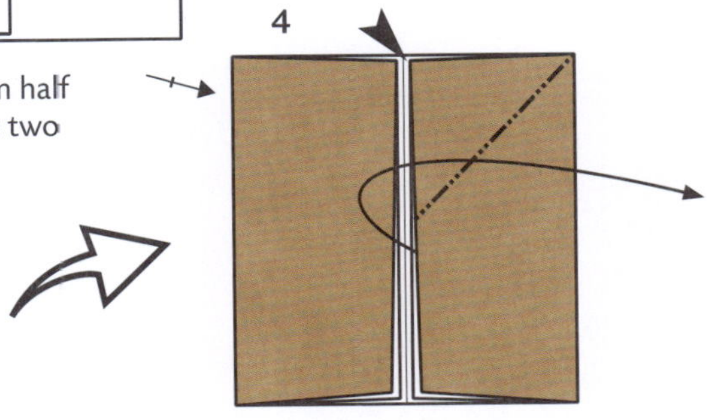

4. This image is enlarged for clarity. Fold back the top left corner of the right flap. Insert your finger through the bottom of the layer you folded back, open it up along the mountain fold, and squash it flat as shown. Repeat on the left side of the model.

7

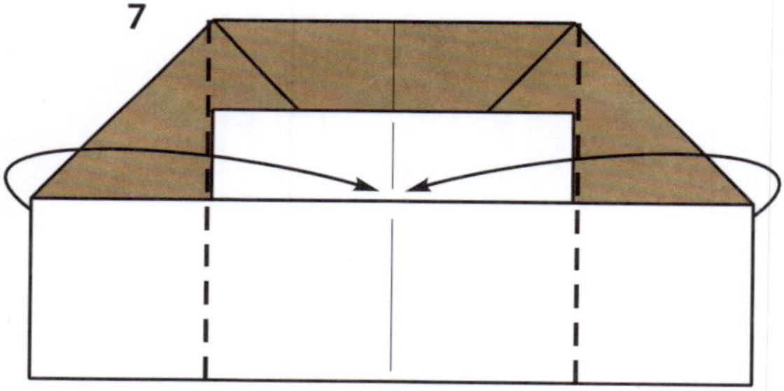

7. Fold the right and left edges inward toward the central axis.

8

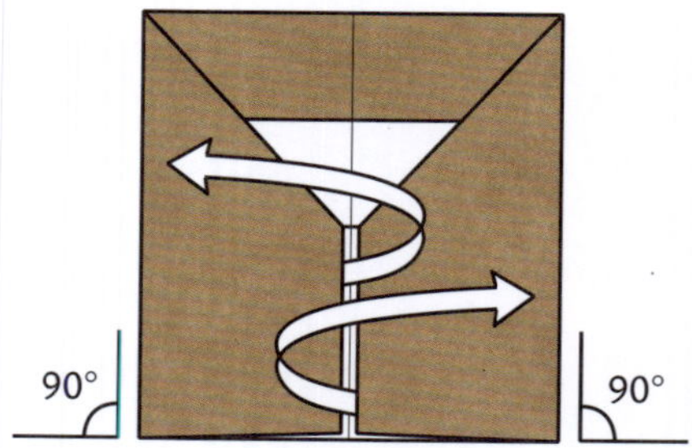

8. Reopen the left and right flaps halfway, so they are at 90° angles to the working surface.

9

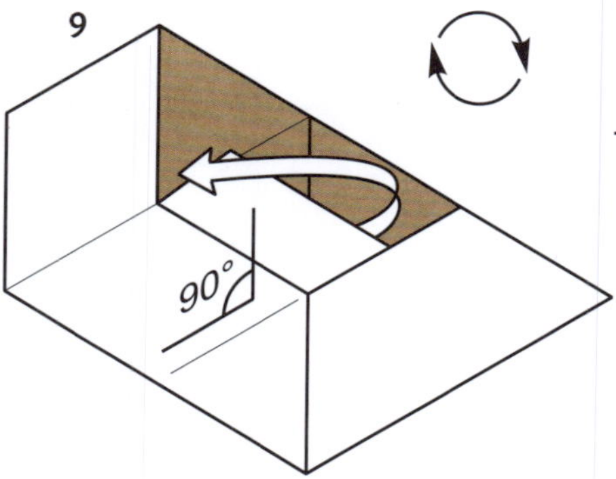

9. Flip the model over so it is lying on its back and lift the central flap vertically, so it is upright relative to the work surface.

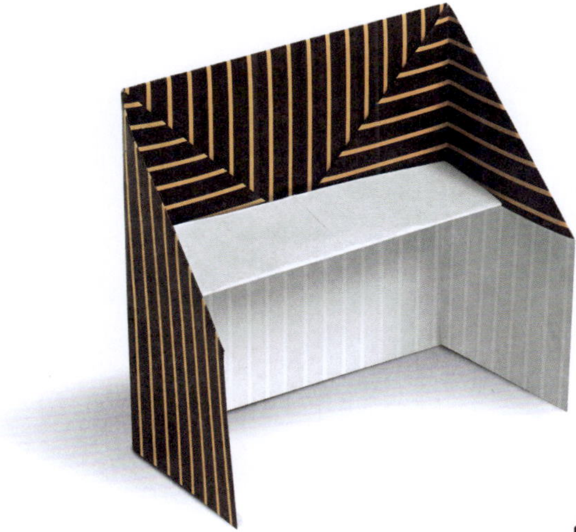

10

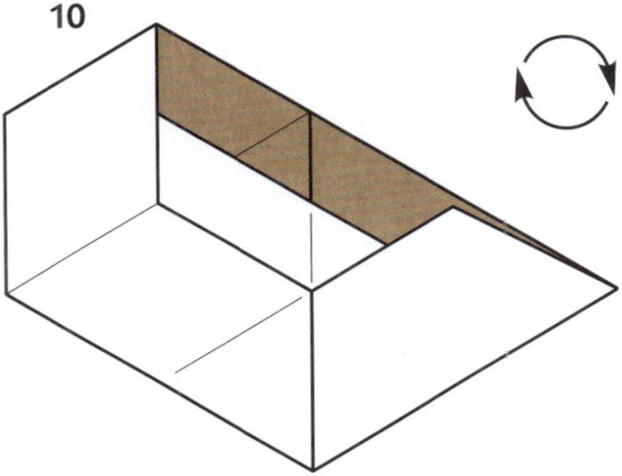

11

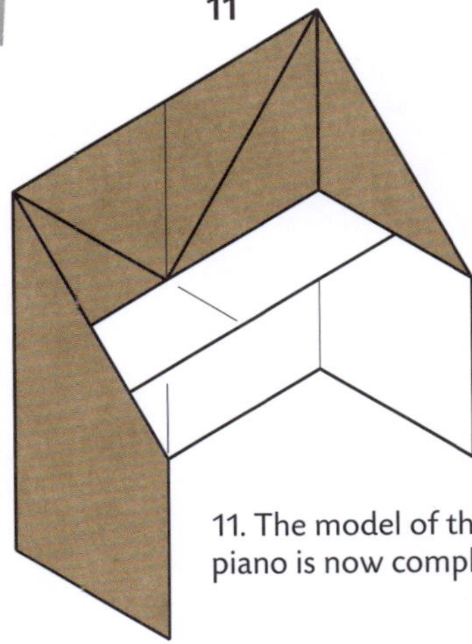

11. The model of the piano is now complete.

10. Flip it up as shown.

Scan for a video tutorial.

Bumblebee

Marc Kirschenbaum

Contrasting stripes are one of the most striking effects one can achieve with origami, and they are all the more extraordinary when you consider they are achieved through a simple series of mountain and valley folds. The bumblebee is characterized by a massive body. For this model, make sure to use paper that has strong, contrasting colors so that once it is complete, the motifs that are most typical of the bumblebee's nature will be readily showcased.

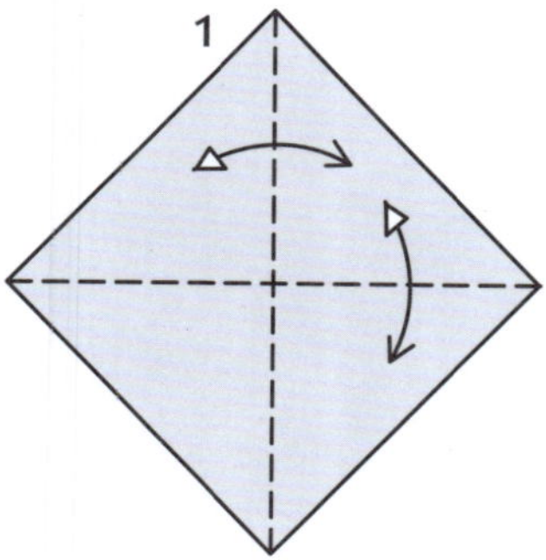

1. Fold the paper in half along both its diagonals and then unfold.

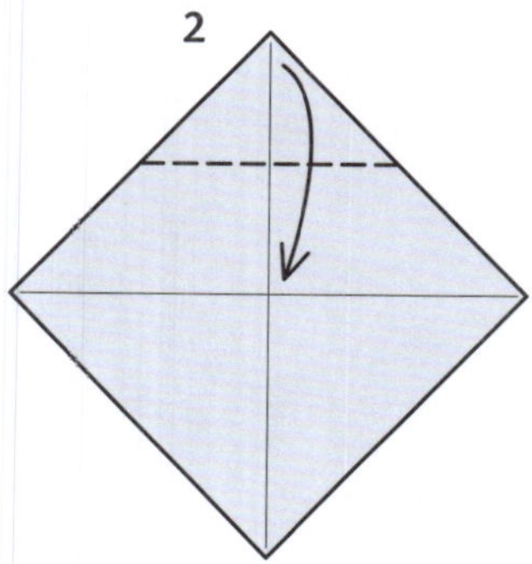

2. Fold the top corner down toward the center.

3

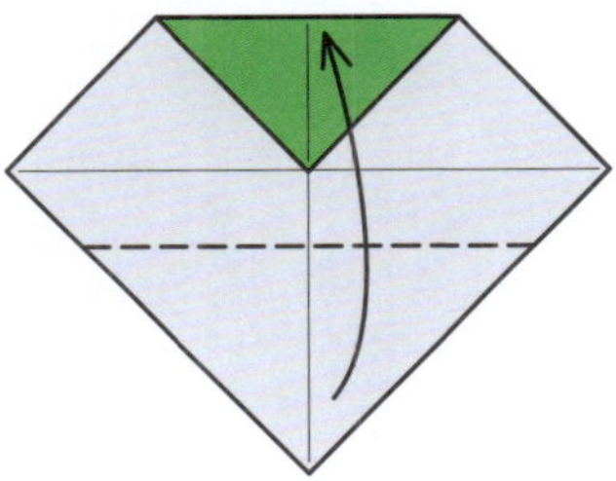

3. Fold the bottom corner upward so the apex meets the top edge of the model.

4

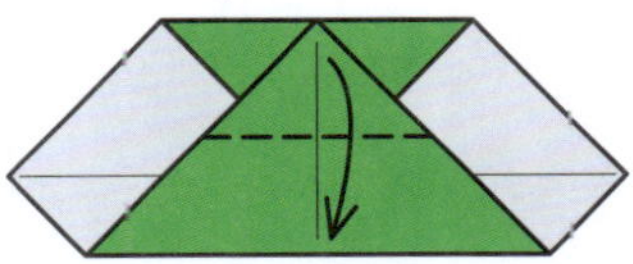

4. Fold the top triangular flap back down, so its point meets the base of the model.

5

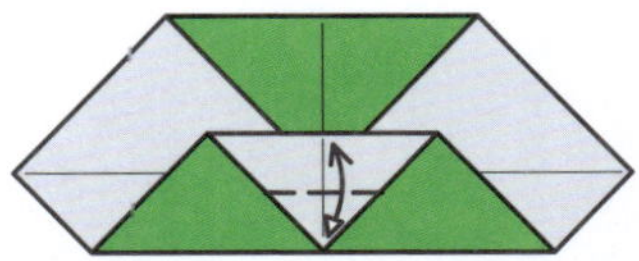

5. Fold the apex of the bottom triangle upward. Crease it and reopen it.

6

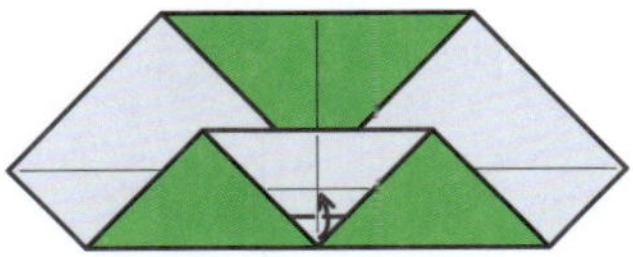

6. Fold the same apex up again, as far as the last crease that was created.

7

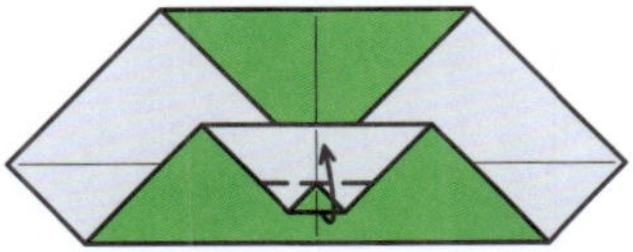

7. Fold the small triangle upward along the existing crease.

8

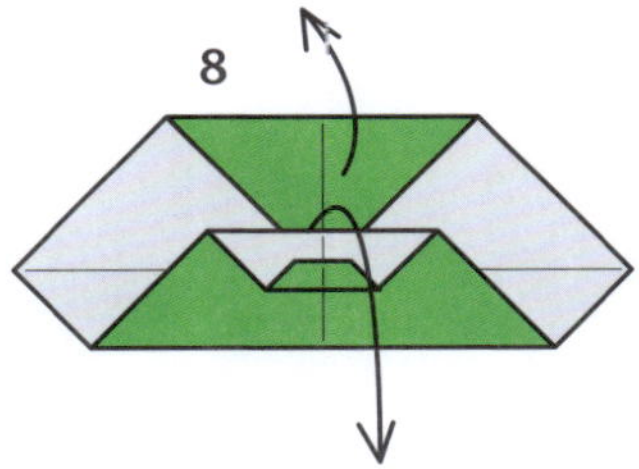

8. Unfold the two flaps.

9

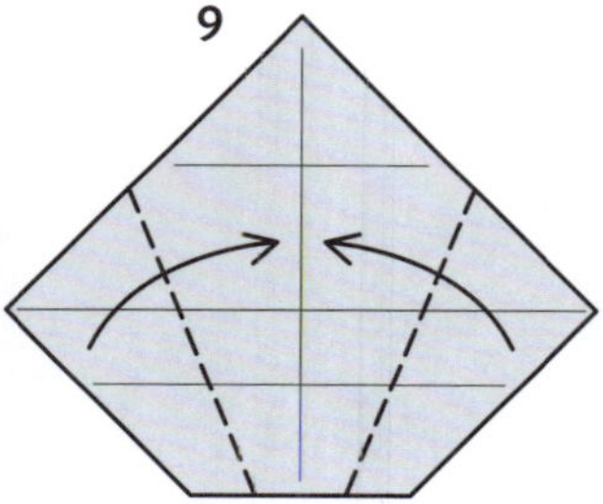

9. Fold the bottom left and bottom right edges inward toward the center.

10

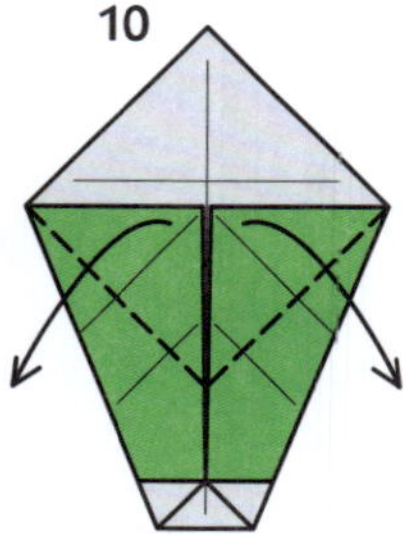

10. Fold the two flaps outward, keeping the side edges straight.

11

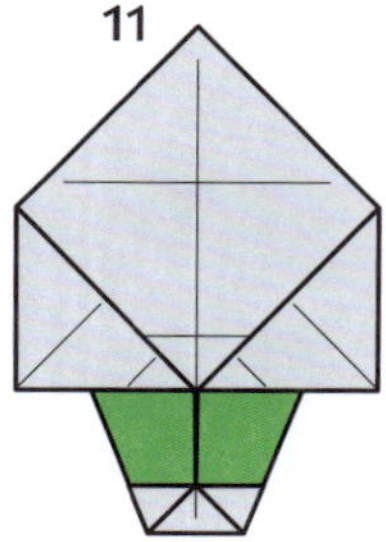

11. Flip the model over.

12

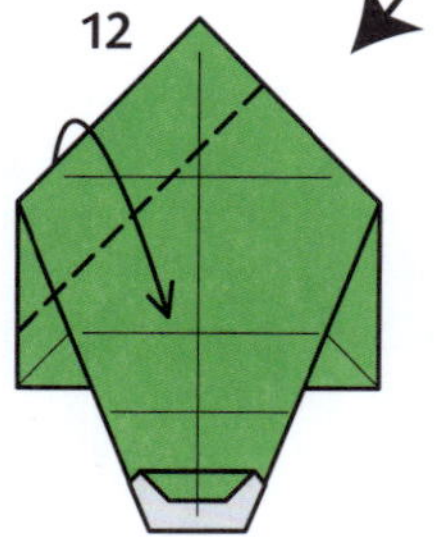

12. Fold the left diagonal edge inward as shown.

13

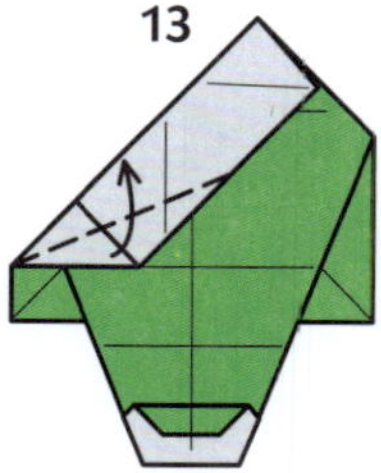

13. Fold the lower, leftmost corner of this flap toward the top edge.

14

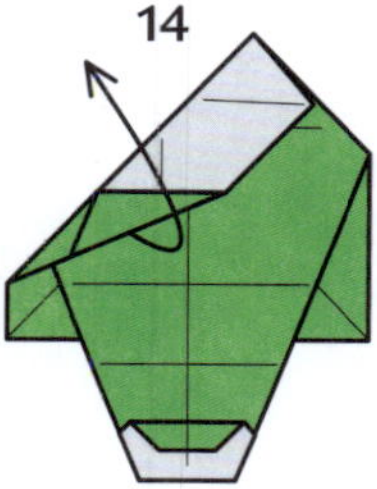

14. Reopen the flap.

15

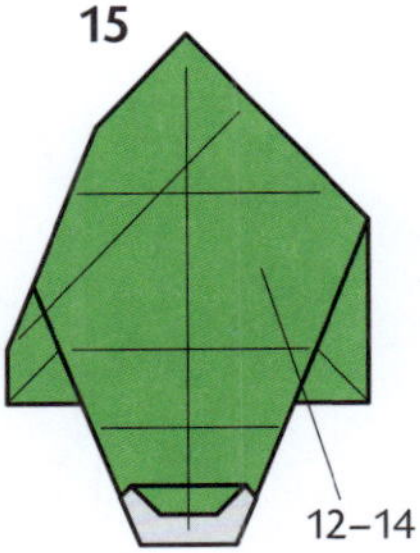

15. Repeat Steps 12–14, in a mirror image fashion, on the right side of the model.

16

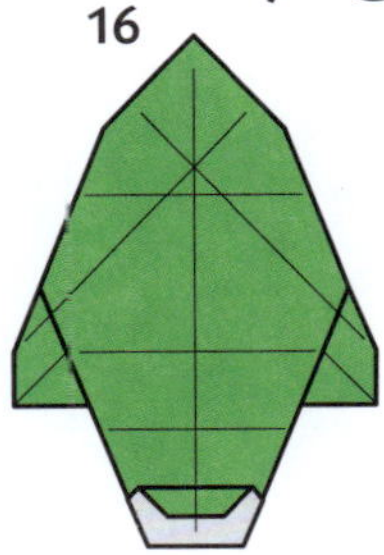

16. Turn the model over.

17

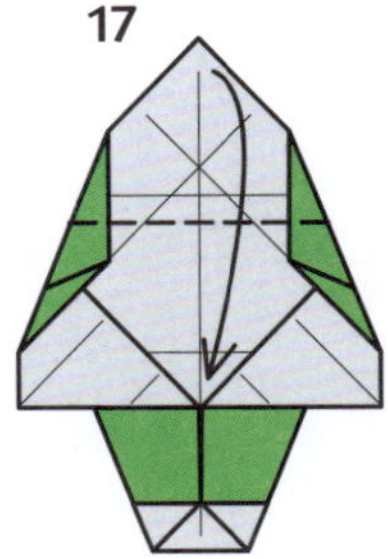

17. Fold the top corner down to the intersection point of all the folds.

18

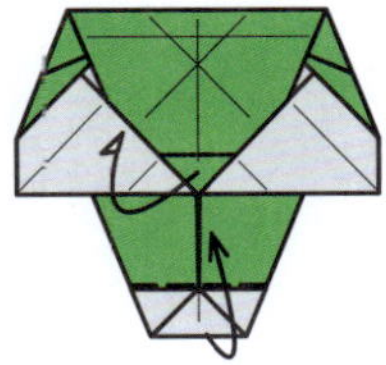

18. Fold the point of the top flap under the flap. Fold the base of the model up as shown.

19

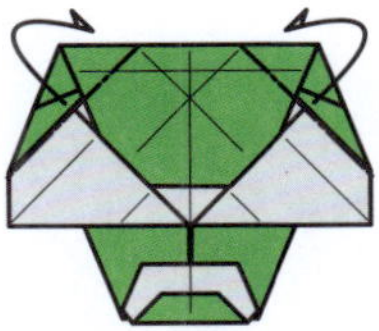

19. Fold the top left and top right corners backward, using mountain folds.

20

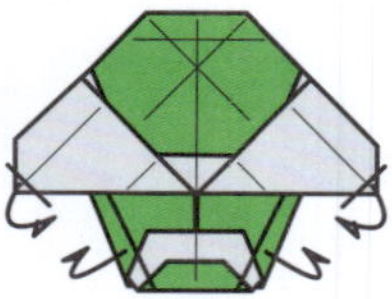

20. Fold back the edges of the abdomen. Fold back the points of the wings.

21

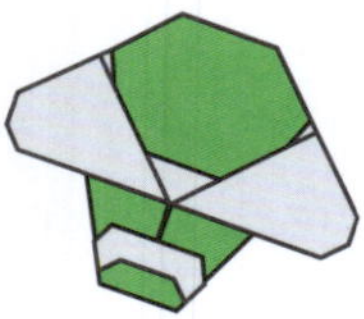

21. The model of the bumblebee is now complete.

Scan for a video tutorial.

Banana

Marc Kirschenbaum

Despite its small size, Costa Rica is rich in natural resources and is a leading exporter of various goods—chief among them, bananas. In fact, all the major banana brands source their product from this country. This origami banana showcases the fruit as it is being peeled.

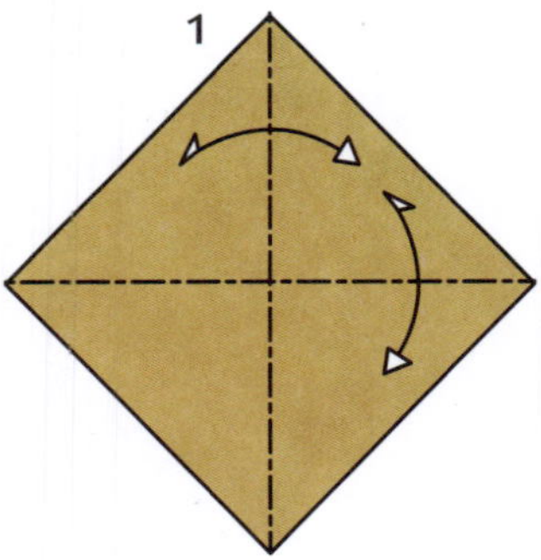

1. Fold the paper in half along both its diagonals using mountain folds, and then unfold.

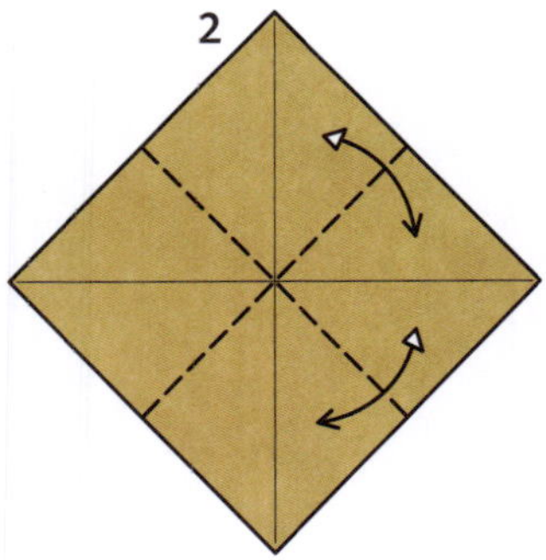

2. Fold the paper in half using the horizontal and vertical median lines, and then unfold.

3

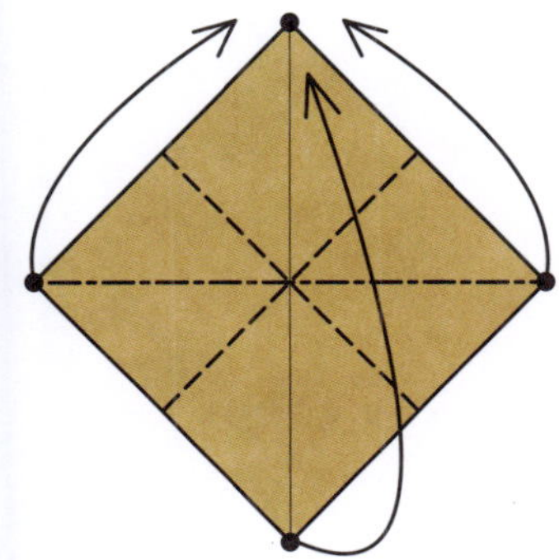

3. Bring the bottom and side corners up to the top, and flatten the model down.

4

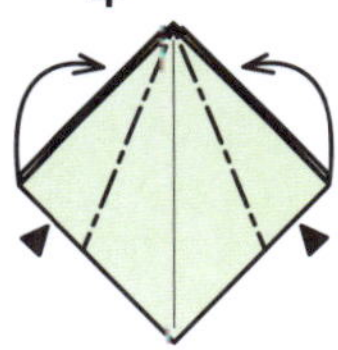

4. Fold the top two side flaps toward the center, then unfold. Then tuck the flaps inward.

5

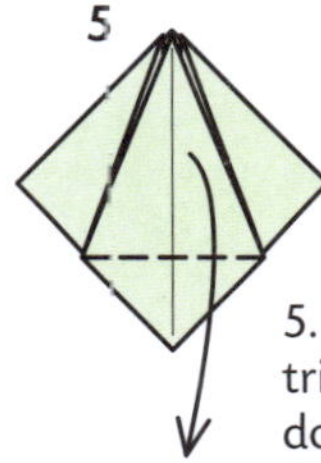

5. Fold the top triangular flap downward, toward the base of the model.

6

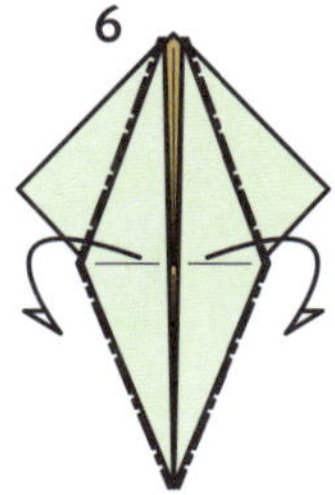

6. Flip each of the two top halves inside out.

7

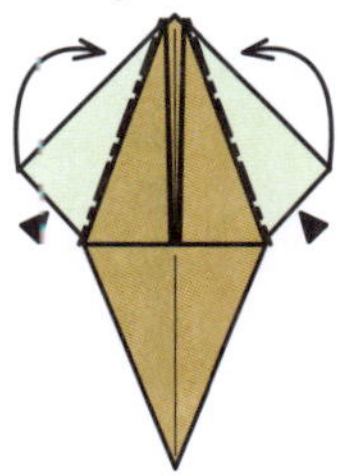

7. Push in the bottom edges of the outer two flaps, collapsing and sinking them inward.

8

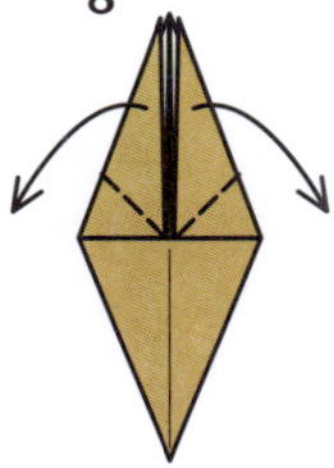

8. Fold the flaps outward.

9

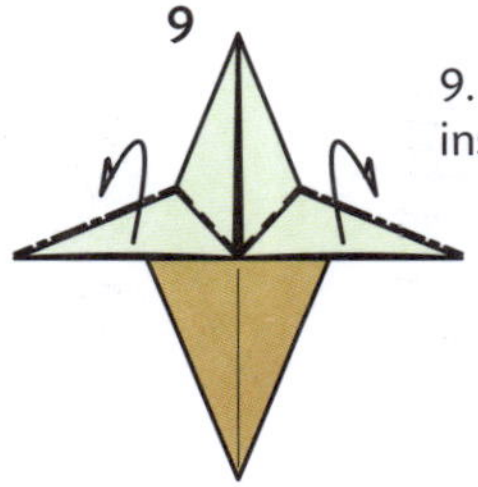

9. Flip the two side flaps inside out.

10

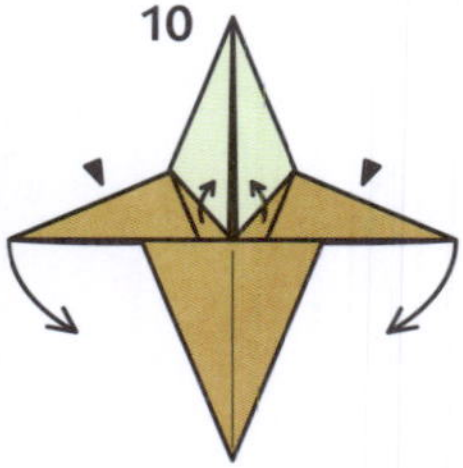

10. Gently flatten the flaps toward the base of the model.

11

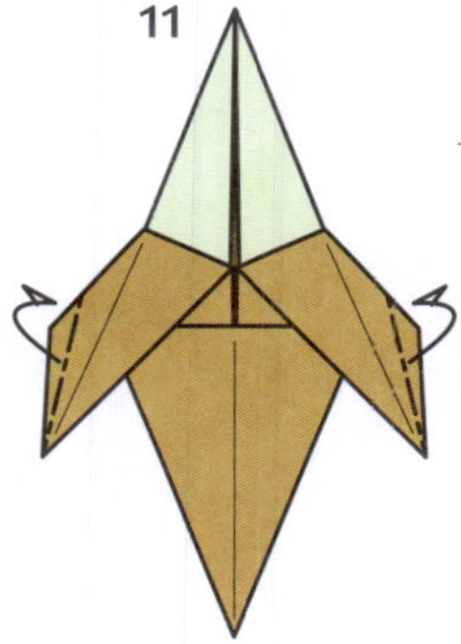

11. Make a mountain fold on each side.

The images have been enlarged to render the folds more visible.

12

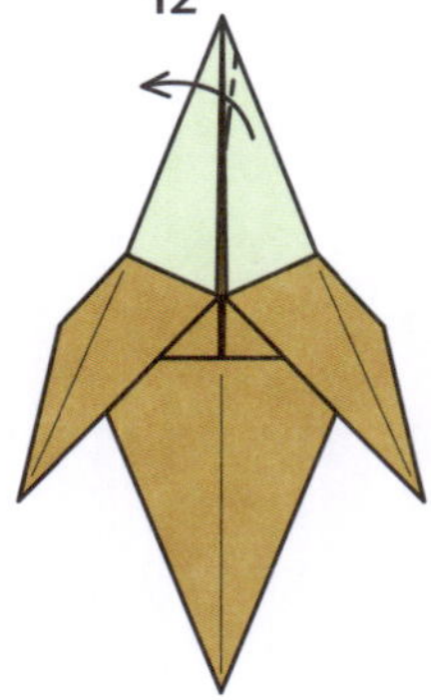

12. Push the top flap forward from the back side and make it slightly convex.

13

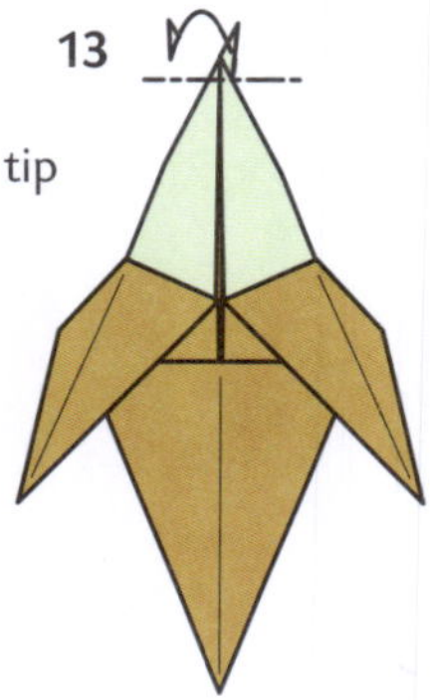

13. Fold the top tip backward.

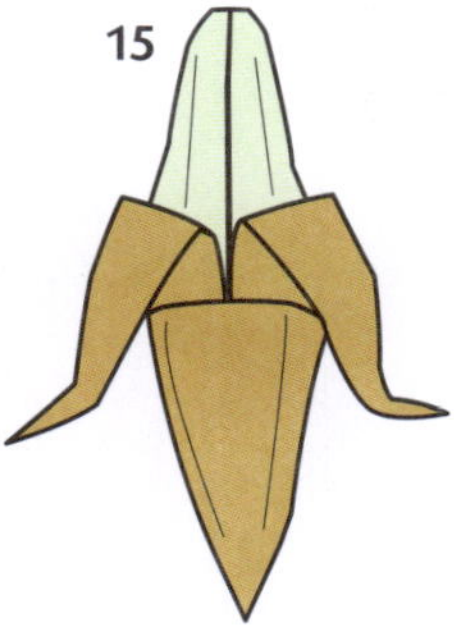

15. The model of the banana is now complete.

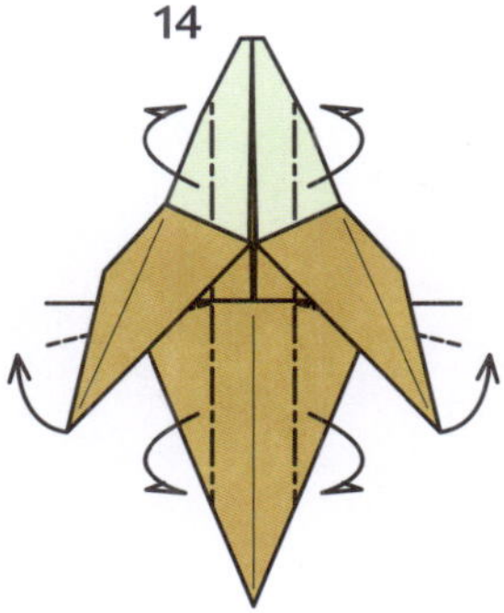

14. Make two additional folds in the bottom part of the model, turning the sides toward the back. Curl the tips of the two side flaps.

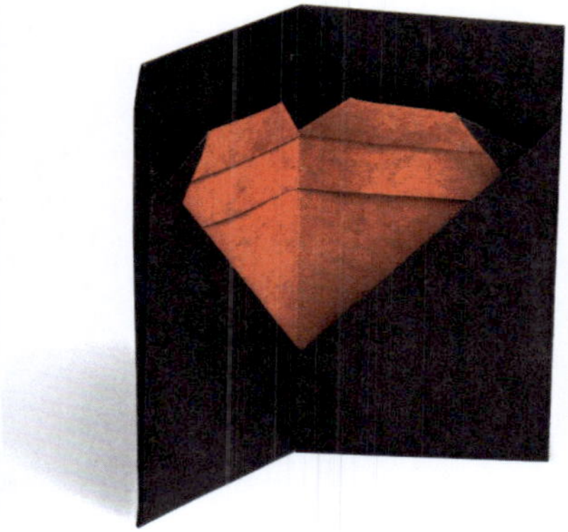

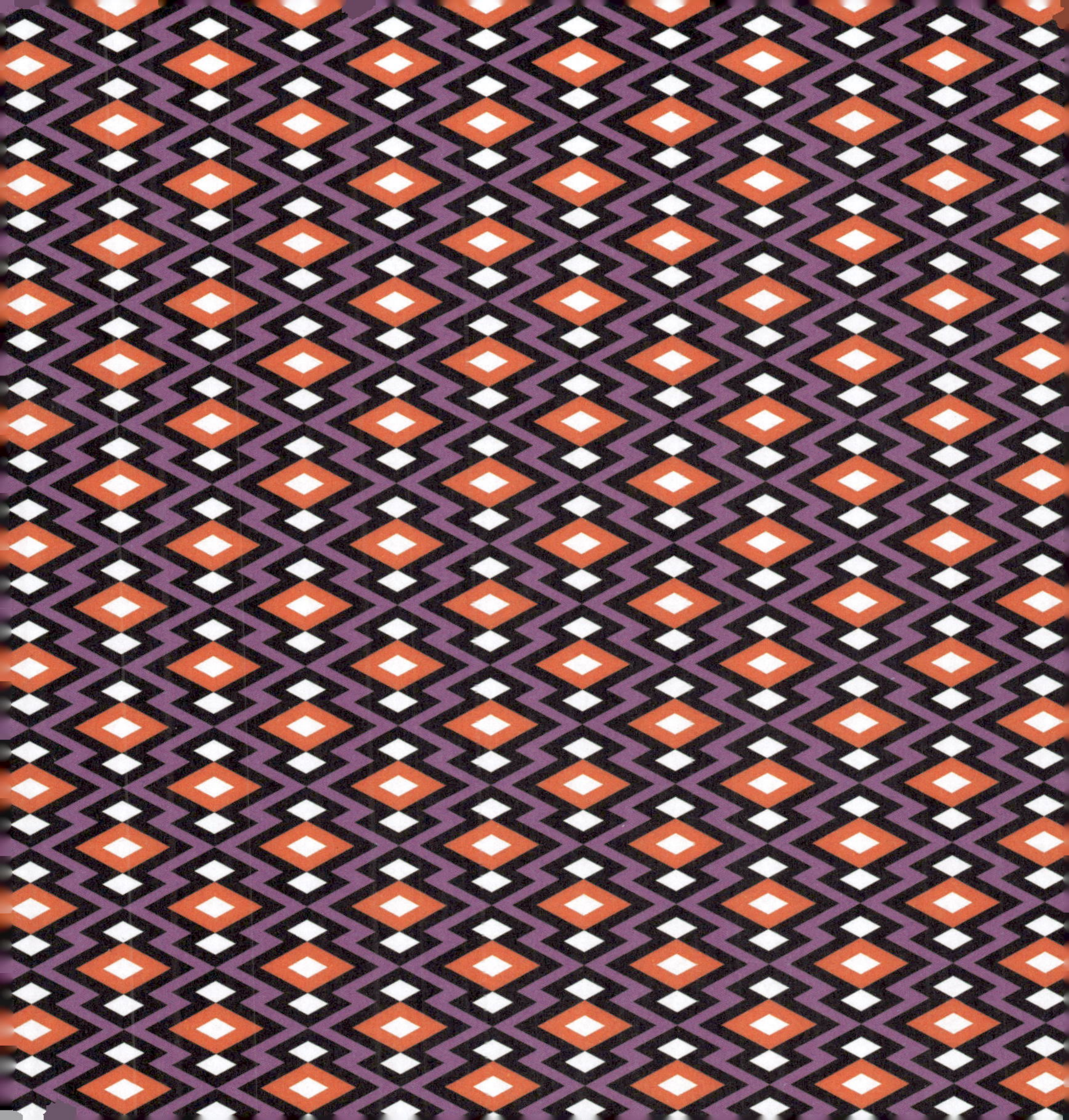

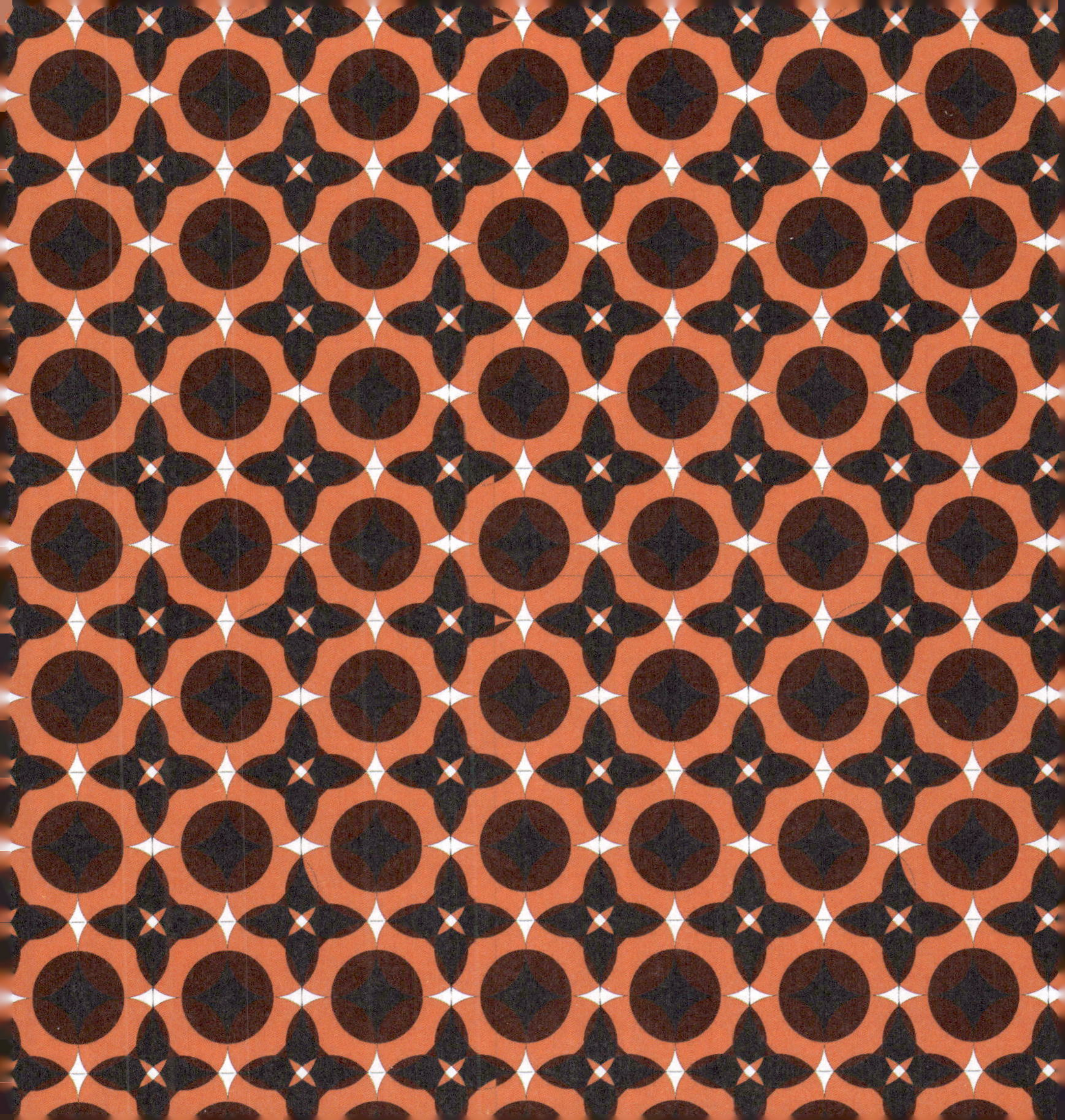

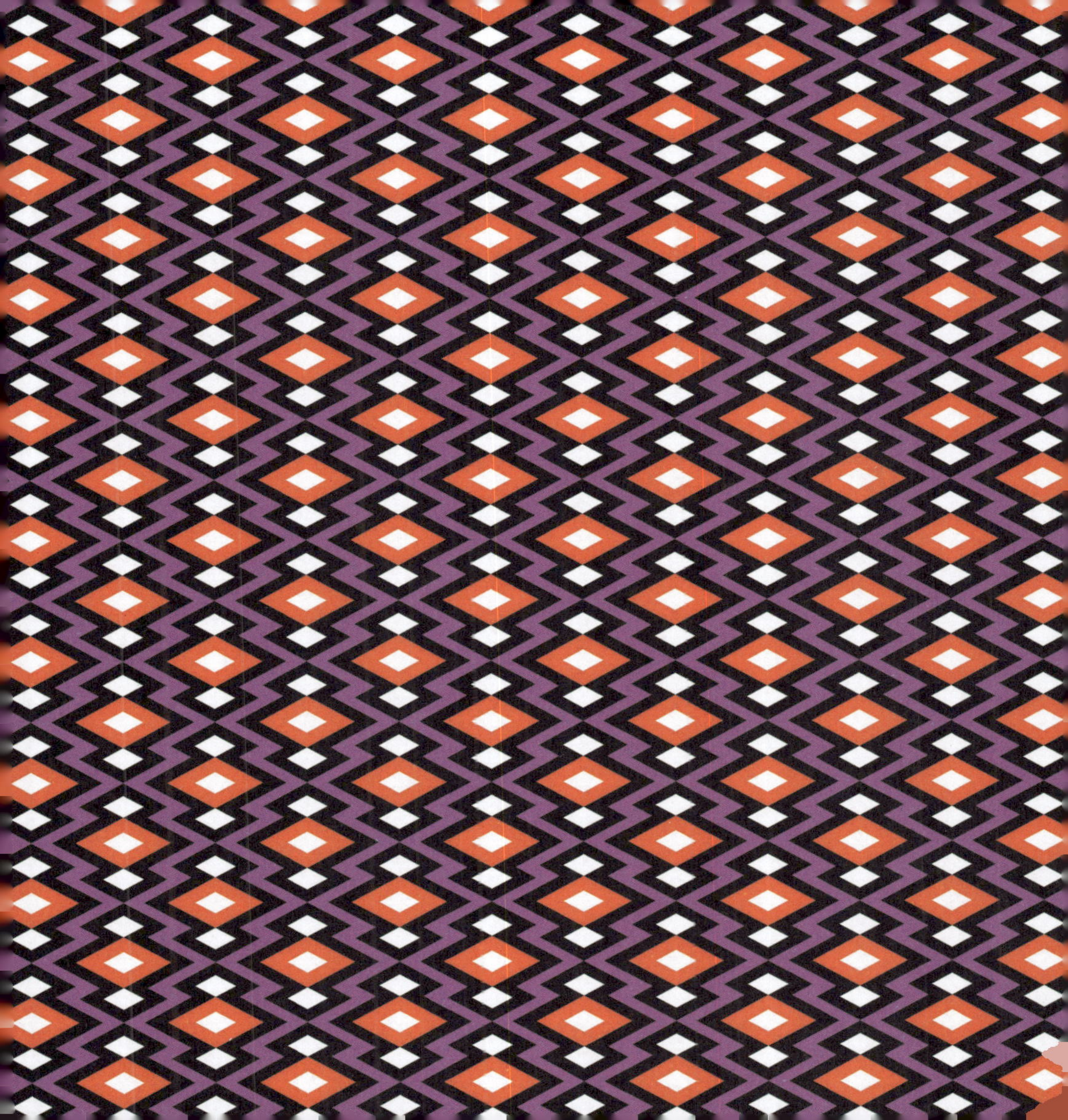

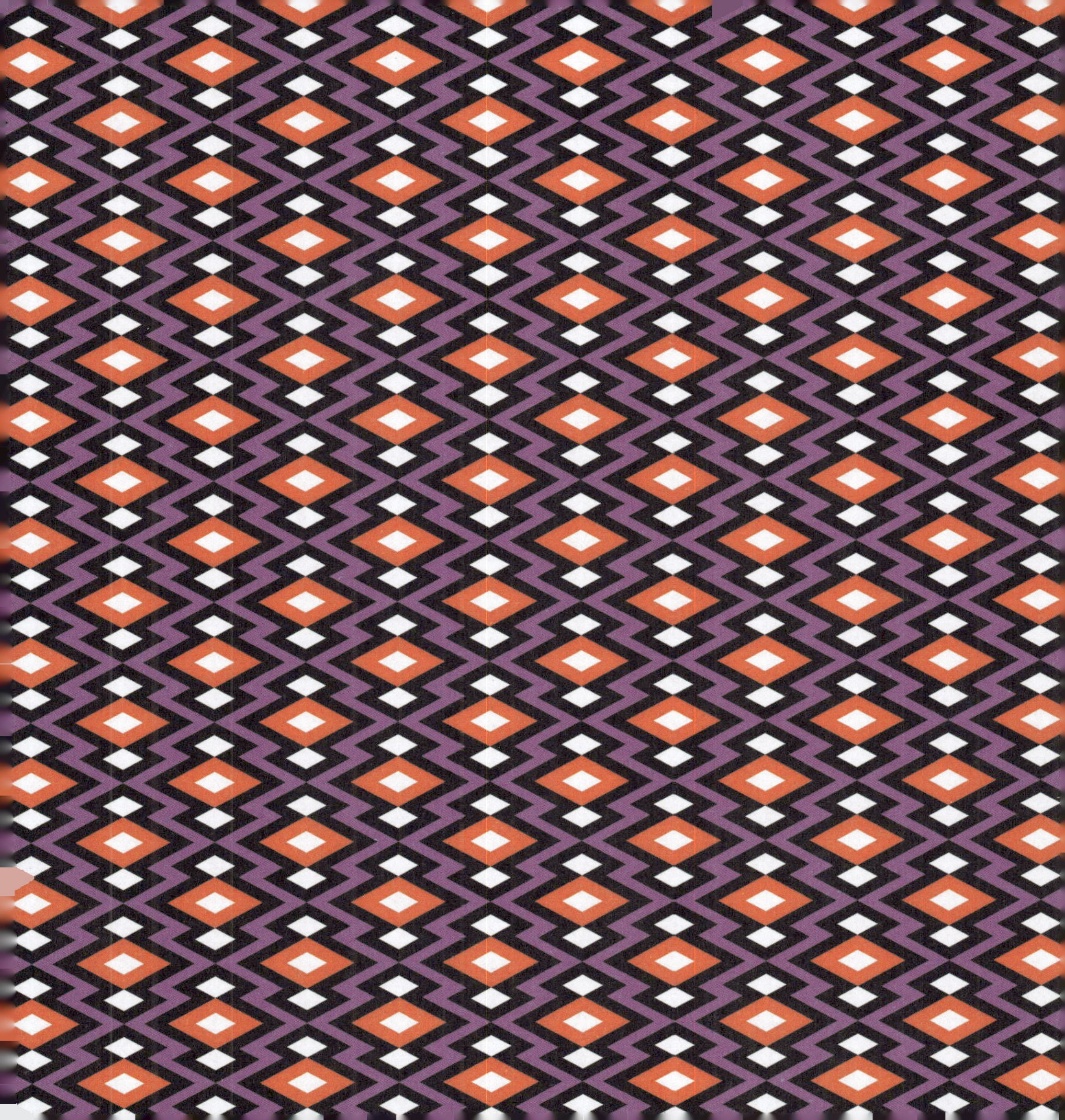

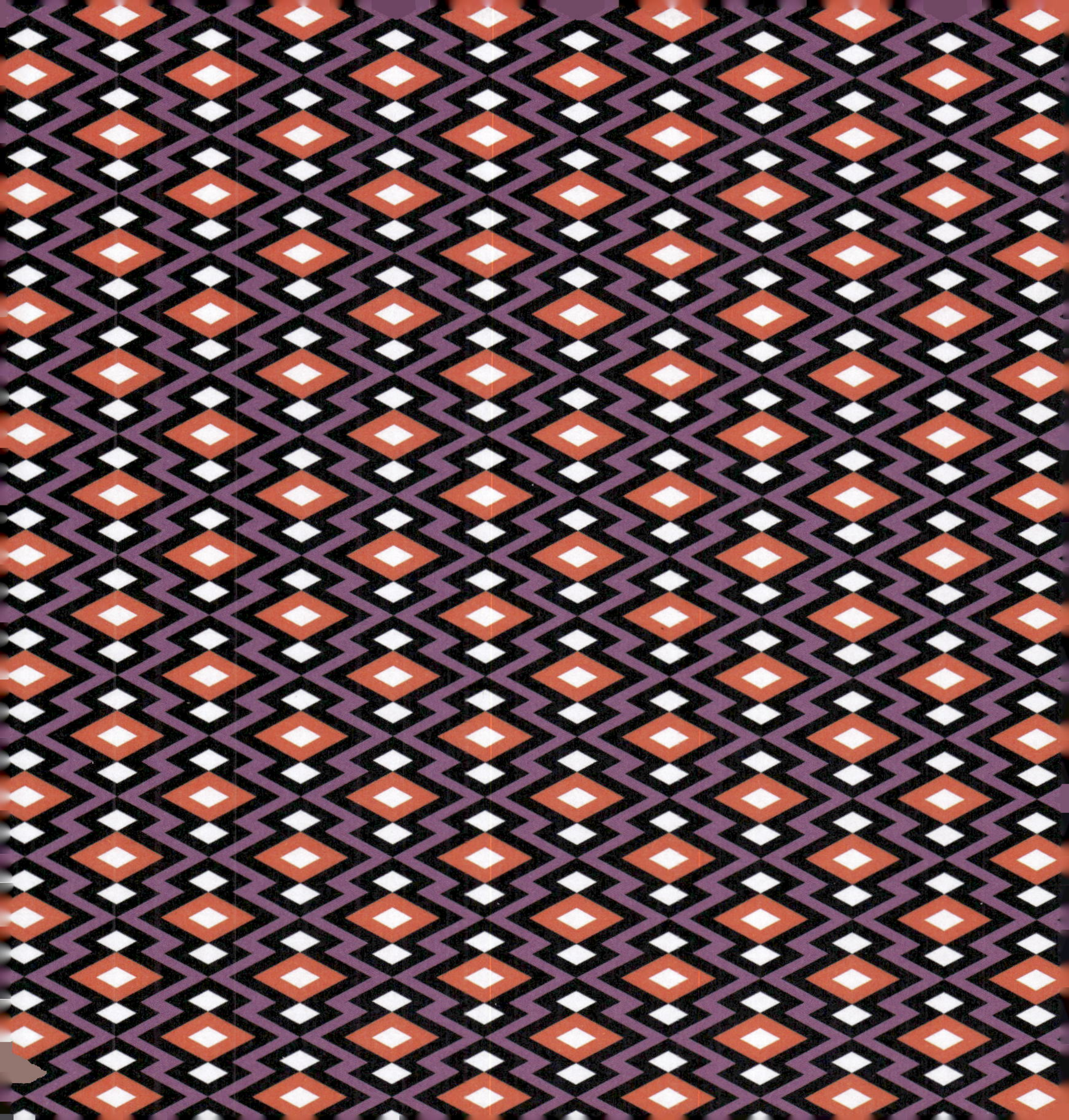